Sweet Eats

Sweet Eats

Mmmore Than Just Desserts

Rose Dunnington

LARK BOOKS

A Division of Sterling Publishing Co., Inc.
New York / London

Editor:
Veronika Alice Gunter

Art Director:
Robin Gregory

Stylist:
Skip Wade

Photographer:
John Widman

Library of Congress Cataloging-in-Publication Data

Dunnington, Rose.
 Sweet eats : mmmore than just desserts / Rose Dunnington. -- 1st ed.
    p. cm.
 ISBN-13: 978-1-60059-236-2 (hc-plc with jacket : alk. paper)
 ISBN-10: 1-60059-236-8 (hc-plc with jacket : alk. paper)
 1. Desserts. 2. Baking. I. Title.
 TX773.D81745 2008
 641.8'6--dc22

                              2007037094

10 9 8 7 6 5 4 3 2 1

First Edition

Published by Lark Books, A Division of
Sterling Publishing Co., Inc.
387 Park Avenue South, New York, NY 10016

Text © 2008, Rose Dunnington
Photography © 2008, Lark Books

Distributed in Canada by Sterling Publishing,
c/o Canadian Manda Group, 165 Dufferin Street
Toronto, Ontario, Canada M6K 3H6

Distributed in the United Kingdom by GMC Distribution Services,
Castle Place, 166 High Street, Lewes, East Sussex, England BN7 1XU

Distributed in Australia by Capricorn Link (Australia) Pty Ltd.,
P.O. Box 704, Windsor, NSW 2756 Australia

The written instructions, photographs, designs, patterns, and projects in this volume are intended for the personal use of the reader and may be reproduced for that purpose only. Any other use, especially commercial use, is forbidden under law without written permission of the copyright holder.

Every effort has been made to ensure that all the information in this book is accurate. However, due to differing conditions, tools, and individual skills, the publisher cannot be responsible for any injuries, losses, and other damages that may result from the use of the information in this book.

If you have questions or comments about this book, please contact:
Lark Books
67 Broadway
Asheville, NC 28801
828-253-0467

Printed in China

ISBN 13: 978-1-60059-236-2
ISBN 10: 1-60059-236-8

For information about custom editions, special sales, premium and corporate purchases, please contact Sterling Special Sales Department at 800-805-5489 or specialsales@sterlingpub.com.

Dedication

For my sweet Papa, John Larston Reitzel

Sweet Eats

The Recipes

Soft Stuff

Munchies

Pie in the Sky

Have Your Cake

Blissful Bites

you *deserve* dessert

When you want something sweet, can you whip up just what you want—when you want it?

This cookbook is all about giving you the skills and the recipes to do just that. Sundaes, cakes, snack bars, cookies, pies, and more—make every kind of sweet eat you could want.

So don't reach for stale, packaged treats with seven-syllable ingredients. And don't wait for someone to make a dessert for you. Get in the kitchen and get cooking! It's fun and way easier than you think. And what you make for yourself and your friends will always taste the best.

When you cook for yourself, you're in control. You can adjust the sweetness and the ingredients to your taste. So, chuck the cherries and pile on the peaches, if you like. Substitute pecans for peanuts so your friends with allergies can enjoy what you're cooking. You'll tempt your friends' and family's taste buds and maybe even show off a little bit.

Homemade sweets are great to share at parties, to give as gifts, or just to treat yourself. You don't need any cooking or baking experience to make my recipes and make them taste great. The book starts with some cooking basics. That's where you'll learn, well, the basics—stuff like reading a recipe and mixing ingredients. I use fresh fruits in many of my recipes, so you'll learn how to peel and cut fruits, among other skills. Just turn to **Getting Started** on page 10 anytime you need a reminder on, say, how to **cream** butter or **zest** fruit. I've also put special cooking terms in bold, so you can look them up in the glossary on page 108.

Then there are the three-dozen plus recipes… Did I mention that your taste buds will take a trip around the world with these recipes? Look for a Spanish flan, Indian rice pudding, Italian spumoni, and Asian flavors in a granita.

If you're counting down the days until the next holiday when someone will bring you something sweet to eat, put away the calendar. Instead, flip through this book, find a recipe, and start a shopping list. It's time you started making some sweet eats.

Getting Started

With so many delicious recipes, the hardest part can be deciding which one to make first.

Having friends over? Look through the **Munchies** and **Blissful Bites** chapters for something to make while you're hanging out. I recommend the Lemon Squares recipe (page 40)—those were a favorite when we took the pictures for this book.

Want something simple but special to share with your family? Check out my recipes for fruit-filled In-a-Skillet Peach Pie (page 70) and Strawberry Sticky (page 68). Serve your family first—you won't forget to put a helping on your plate! Desserts this good are always gone before you know it.

The **Have Your Cake** chapter is full of ideas for what to make for a celebration, like a birthday. But be sure to consider the birthday boy's or girl's taste—my papa loves pie, so he gets a birthday pie instead of a cake.

When you pick out a recipe, you should always think about who will be eating your delectable creation. If you're going to share with a whole bunch of people, avoid recipes with nuts—some people are allergic. Nuts aren't so great for babies or older people who don't have all of their teeth, either. You also might want to think about the time of year. Green Tea and Honeydew Granita (page 36) is cooling in the summer, and Apple Spice Cake (page 76) is cozy in the fall or winter.

After you choose what you want to make, read the recipe all the way through. Check to see if you have everything you need and enough time to finish. Create a shopping list for anything you must buy. Each recipe includes a **yield**, which tells you how much food each recipe makes. If you're unsure of any terms, check back in this section or turn to the Glossary (pages 108-109).

Ready to get in the kitchen? Wash your hands, tie back your hair if it's long, and put on an apron if you want. Remove rings, bracelets, and watches. (The windowsill is a better spot for them than the edge of the sink. I think you can guess why.)

Mise en Place

Now it's time to put everything in its place. That's **mise en place** (say it MEEZ-ahn-plahs) in French chef-speak. Basically, it means that you get your **ingredients** and **equipment** ready before you start cooking. Think of mise en place as the backstage work for a cooking show.

So, look at the ingredient and equipment lists for a recipe you want to make. Arrange all of those items on the countertop.

I like to put my ingredients all together to the left of my workspace. Once I've added something to the recipe, I move the box or bag to the right. This way, I don't get confused about whether I've already added an ingredient.

Each recipe in this book has a list of everything you'll use, and now's the time to make sure your measuring cups aren't lost or dirty. If your kitchen equip-

ment isn't exactly like what the list calls for, that's okay. For example, a 2½-quart pot works just as well as a 2-quart pot. Turn to the Equipment Glossary on page 106 if you want to see examples of the equipment you'll use.

To finish your mise en place, make sure that the sink is empty and the dishwasher, trash can, and compost bin have room. I know it's a pain, but cleanup is part of cooking. If you start with a tidy kitchen, it will only take a few minutes to get it back that way when you're done.

Prepping

You'll notice that some of the ingredients have **prep** instructions, such as "butter, softened." Prepping ranges from **sifting** flour to washing, peeling,

and slicing apples. It's all fun. Especially with friends.

If liquid ingredients need to be heated, such as cream for Truffles on page 104, do it in the microwave. You can **soften** butter in the microwave, too, but make sure you do it on low power and check the butter's progress every 5 seconds. Often, the center of a stick will melt before the outside is soft; cut the butter into chunks to avoid this. An even easier way to soften butter is to take it out of the fridge and let it sit on the counter for an hour or so.

If an ingredient should be cold, stick it in the freezer while you collect everything else you need.

Wash and dry all **produce** in a **colander** before you use it.

A.

Plain water usually does the trick, but you can use a tiny drop of dish soap if you make sure to rinse well. **Pick over** a colander full of berries to remove any stray leaves or bad berries before you wash them.

Use a knife and **cutting board** to chop or slice fruit. Make a claw out of the hand that you don't write with, tucking the thumb behind the fingertips. (It will look kind of like the letter "e" in sign language.) Use that claw to hold down the food you're cutting. The thumb can guide the food forward, as long as it stays behind the fingers.

B.

C.

D.

Never raise the blade (the cutting edge) of the knife higher than the knuckles of your guiding hand.

Some fruits require special techniques for slicing or dicing. A large, flat pit runs through the center of a mango. To dice the mango, you must first cut to either side of the pit (shown in the lower left corner of photo A.) Then, use a table knife to cut a grid pattern in the flesh of each mango half. Turn each half inside out so it looks like a porcupine. (See photo A.) Knock the mango chunks out to use them in the recipe.

You'll peel most thin-skinned fruits with a **vegetable peeler**. Always peel away from your body—the blade is sharp.

To peel and slice kiwis, you'll need a **paring knife**, a spoon, and the fruit. Use the knife to cut off the kiwi's ends. Then slide the spoon down into either end of the kiwi, between the fruit's flesh and its peel. Work the spoon around to remove the peel. Then cut the kiwi into thin slices. (See photo B.)

You can use a spoon to **hull** strawberries. (See photo C.) After removing the stems and leaves, use a paring knife to slice the strawberries.

Melons have a thick **rind**. So you remove the fruit with a paring knife. (See photo D.)

If you're working with a fruit that requires special handling, the recipe includes instructions and how-to photos to guide you.

Most importantly, always take your time and pay attention—some foods like juicy peaches can be slippery! If someone starts talking to you while you're using a sharp tool, put it down. Then have your conversation.

E.

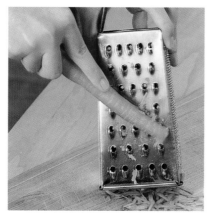

F.

G.

Speaking of peaches, to prep a peach, you typically need to peel it, pit it, and slice it. To do this, grab a vegetable peeler, a paring knife, and a peach.

Hold the peach firmly in your non-dominant hand. Use your other hand to place the peeler's blade at the top of the fruit. Sink the blade in just below the peel. Pull the peeler toward you in a controlled motion. (See photo E.) Continue working your way all around the fruit until you've removed all of its peel.

To slice it, begin by cutting the peach in half with the par-

ing knife. The knife will hit the peach's pit, so you must carefully work the knife in a straight line around the fruit. When you've cut all the way around, put down the knife.

Pull the halves of the peach apart. Remove the pit with your fingers. Slice the peach. Done!

Grating is another way of cutting an ingredient. For most foods, use a box-shaped **grater**. Push the food against the grater in a downward motion. On the upward motion, don't press down. Repeat lots of times. (See photo F.)

Zest citrus fruits on the small holes of the box grater, or use a microplane grater like you see in photo G. Just grate the colored part of the rind to cut it into little pieces called zests. The white part tastes bitter.

You don't just prep your ingredients. You also need to set out and be ready to use any appliances, baking pans, or other equipment called for in the recipe you've chosen.

A **food processor** comes in handy for chopping and grinding nuts for Honey-Nut Baklava (page 96) and mixing dough

H.

I.

for Primo Piecrust (page 58). The creamed fruit desserts on page 24 are made in a **blender**.

Get an adult to show you exactly how your **appliances** work. Always unplug your blender or food processor before you reach inside it.

When a recipe calls for a **greased** pan, you need to apply butter, oil, or cooking spray to the pan. The "grease" will make sure your goodies release from the pan after baking. I like to grease a pan by rubbing it with the inside of a

butter wrapper. (See photo H.) Be sure to get the butter spread in all the corners. Your hands stay clean (mostly) and the pan is well-greased.

If the recipe doesn't call for butter, I usually use unflavored cooking spray. Hold your breath while you spray!

Cakes need something to grab onto while they rise in the oven, so you should **flour** a cake pan after you grease it. Sprinkle flour in the greased pan and shake it around until the bottom and sides are coated. (See photo I.) Dump out the extra flour.

Measuring

It's important to use the right amount of each ingredient to get your recipe right. Easy-peasy! Just use **liquid measuring cups** for liquids, such as milk, and **solid measuring cups** for solids, such as flour. **Measuring spoons** work for both liquids and solids.

Liquid measuring cups usually have tons of lines, numbers, and abbreviations, such as ml and oz. Figure out which line marks the measurement you want, and pour up to that line.

The best way to get an accurate measurement is to put the cup on a stable surface and align your eyes with the top of the liquid.

Some solid measuring cups have lines, too, but it's best to use the scoop that perfectly measures the amount you want. Dip your scoop into the ingredient, and then move the flat edge of a knife across the rim of the cup to push the extra off the top. If you use flour straight from the bag, stir it up first to get the lumps out.

Brown sugar and coconut should be **packed** in the measuring cup. (See photo J.) All other ingredients are measured in their natural, fluffy state.

It may seem like the amounts of **baking powder** and **baking soda** are too tiny to do anything. Don't be fooled! These are very powerful ingredients.

J.

Too much leaves a nasty taste in your goodies; too little makes them flat and dense.

I'll let you in on a secret: Except for baking powder and baking soda, a little bit more or less of an ingredient won't drastically change your finished dessert. If I have half of a carrot left over after grating the 4 cups I need for carrot cake, I go ahead and use the rest. If I only have 1¾ cups of pecans, the pecan tart tastes fabulous, even though the recipe calls for 2 cups.

You'll notice that some fruity recipes give a range for

K.

the amount of sugar. This is because the only way to measure how much sweetness the fruit adds to the recipe is to taste it. You may think the sweeter the better, but too much sugar takes away from the flavor of the fruit.

To judge how much sugar to use, first mix in the smallest amount. Have a taste, and gradually add more sugar until you find the perfect balance of sweet and tart.

Mixing
The way ingredients are mixed makes a huge difference in

L.

M.

N.

your final dessert. Perfect Pound Cake (page 78) would be more like hockey puck cake without all the **beating** you see in the recipe's instructions.

There are lots of different ways to mix ingredients. Do your best to use the mixing technique called for in the recipe you're following. The most common one is **stirring**—making circles in a bowl with a spoon. (See photo K.)

Sometimes you need to do more. Here are some other mixing terms that I use:

Beat with an **electric mixer**, **whisk**, or fork. If you're using a whisk or fork, make small fast circles with your wrist. Bring the **utensil** partially above the surface of the food so that air gets in the food.

Whipping is a faster, longer form of beating. It adds lots of air to whatever you are mixing, which allows you to make deliciously fluffy stuff like whipped cream. I recommend using an electric mixer for whipping. (See photo L.)

Cream softened butter and sugar with an electric mixer

or fork. The mixture will get fluffy and lighter in color, and you will no longer see or feel individual sugar granules. (See photo M.)

Remember to always unplug your electric mixer before changing the attachments, cleaning it, or—my favorite— licking the beaters.

Fold ingredients into batter with a **rubber spatula**. Use a sideways stirring motion—think Ferris wheel. Scrape the batter from the bottom of the bowl and let it fall over the new ingredients. (See photo N.)

Cooking Up Hot Stuff

A handful of these recipes require stovetop cooking. Make sure you have an adult's permission before you get started. Then choose a pot that will be about halfway full when you put your ingredients in it. (Unless, of course, the recipe says to use an even bigger pot.) Aim pot handles toward the middle of the stove. Wear **oven mitts** for moving hot pots and lifting lids.

A couple of recipes will ask you to **boil** ingredients. Boiling happens when a liquid gets hot enough to turn into steam. There are lots of rolling bubbles. (See photo O.)

Simmering is a mini version of boiling. Tiny bubbles come to the surface of a liquid while it cooks at a steady, medium heat. Your stove may simmer at a lower setting; be sure to watch how the food cooks.

O.

More than half of these recipes involve **baking**. Baking is easy—you put the food in the oven and walk away, and it does the work. But you have to get a few things just right.

Heat comes from the bottom of the oven when it bakes. Since heat rises, the food gets cooked from all directions. **Preheating** gets the oven to the temperature needed for your desserts. Make sure there's a rack in the middle of the oven before you preheat.

Put the prepared food in the center of that middle rack.

P.

That's because you want to bake your marvelous creations as close to the center of the oven as you can for the most even cooking. Otherwise, you'll notice that your cakes are really flat on one side or your cupcakes might point up on one side. (See photo P.)

Always wear oven mitts when you take things out of the oven. And remember, the door and sides of the oven are hot, too. So, keep your hands and arms away from them. Have a **hot pad** or **trivet** ready to put hot baking dishes on.

The Recipes

Okay, are you ready to make something yummy? Go for it! Oh, one last tip: Try not to drool on the book.

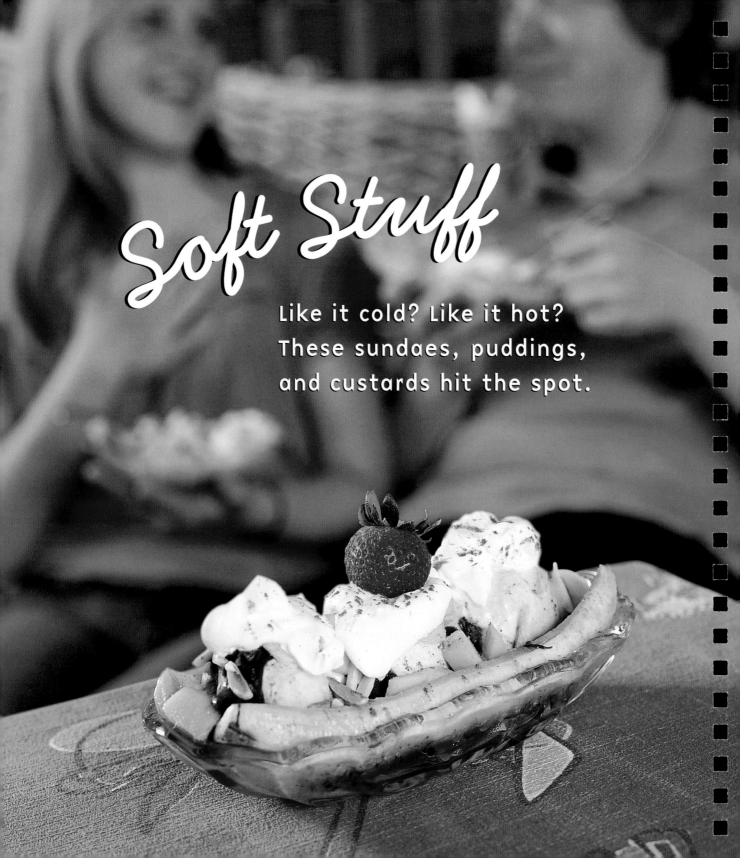

Soft Stuff

Like it cold? Like it hot? These sundaes, puddings, and custards hit the spot.

Plantain
Ice Cream Split

A plantain is like a banana—but not! Fry one for a super-terrific flavor that livens up an old-fashioned dessert.

Equipment
- skillet • spatula • bowl • measuring cups and spoons • serving dish

Ingredients
- handful of slivered almonds
- about 1 teaspoon cooking oil, such as canola
- 1 plantain (the blacker the better), peeled and halved lengthwise
- 3 scoops ice cream (I like coffee-flavored. Strawberry and vanilla are also yummy.)
- ¼ cup Hot Mama Fudge sauce (recipe next page)
- 1 mango, pitted, peeled, and diced (See page 13.)
- dollop of whipped cream (recipe next page)
- cinnamon
- 1 strawberry

Makes: one dessert—enough for two or three people to share

From putting ingredients on the kitchen counter to taking your first bite, you'll need about 20 minutes.

1 Toast the almonds in the dry skillet over medium heat, stirring occasionally. When the almonds are lightly brown, use the spatula to scoop them into a bowl.

2 Put enough oil in the empty skillet to lightly coat the bottom. Sauté the plantain halves for 5 minutes per side, until golden brown.

3 Construct your split: Put the sautéed plantains in the bottom of your serving dish. Add ice cream. Top it with Hot Mama Fudge and diced mango. Dollop on whipped cream, and scatter the toasted almonds over the whole dessert. Finish with a sprinkle of cinnamon and a strawberry on top of the whipped cream. The plantain will be so deliciously soft you can cut it with a spoon.

continued on next page

Hot Mama Fudge

Makes: about 1 cup
This hot fudge sauce takes 15 to 20 minutes to prepare.

Ingredients

- 2 ounces (2 squares) unsweetened baking chocolate
- ⅓ cup water
- ½ stick (¼ cup) butter
- 3 tablespoons cocoa powder
- ¾ cup sugar
- ¼ cup corn syrup (Grease the measuring cup so that the syrup doesn't stick to it.)
- ⅛ teaspoon salt
- ½ teaspoon vanilla extract

Equipment

- measuring cups and spoons
- small sauce pot
- wooden spoon or heat-proof rubber spatula

1 Melt the chocolate, water, butter, and cocoa powder over medium heat, stirring constantly. Add the sugar, corn syrup, vanilla extract, and salt. Stir until the sugar dissolves.

2 Stop stirring. I mean it—take the spoon out of the pot. When the mixture comes to a boil, reduce the heat to medium-low. Keep an eye on it—you want it to boil, but not spatter. Boil 7 to 10 minutes, until thick. (How will you know it's thick if you're not allowed to stir? Swirl the pot.)

3 Let the sauce cool a little bit—you want to eat it hot, not boiling. (It will thicken as it cools.) Store in a sealed container in the fridge for up to one month. Reheat extra sauce in the microwave.

Whipped Cream

Makes: about 6 big scoops
You can make whipped cream in less than 5 minutes.

Ingredients

- ½ pint heavy whipping cream
- 1 tablespoon sugar
- ½ teaspoon vanilla extract

Equipment

- measuring spoons
- mixing bowl
- electric mixer

1 Combine the whipping cream, sugar, and vanilla extract in a mixing bowl. Whip until stiff. Voilà. Homemade whipped cream!

Fast, Fresh, Fruit Creamies

Have some fruit in the fridge? Want a light, creamy dessert—right this second? This blend-it, eat-it recipe is just for you.

Equipment

• paring knife • measuring cups • blender

Ingredients

• 1 pound strawberries, peaches, kiwis, mangos, or any combination of soft fruits, chilled

• ¼ to ½ cup sugar, depending on how sweet your fruit is

• 1 cup whipping cream

Makes: about 6 servings

Layer this dessert with granola in a tall glass and you've just made parfaits!

The blending only takes a couple minutes. Prepping the fruits takes about 5 minutes. For the creamiest dessert, chill the prepped fruit for a minimum of 15 minutes.

1 Hull the strawberries; peel, pit, and slice the peaches; peel and slice the kiwis; and pit, peel, and slice the mangos. (See pages 12, 13, and 14 for tips.)

2 If you want, save a few pieces of fruit for garnish like you see in the photo. Put the rest in the blender. Press purée and let the blender do the work. You want the fruit to be pulverized to a liquid.

3 Now add the sugar and whipping cream, and blend until the whole concoction is creamy. Serve in bowls with spoons and enjoy. Cover and refrigerate leftovers for up to 3 days.

Try a pop:
Pour into freezer molds. Tap the molds on the counter to get rid of air bubbles. Freeze for 2 hours.

Try a pie:
Using a metal pie plate, pile the creamy goodness in a graham cracker crust (page 61). Freeze for 2 hours. (Use a metal pie plate because glass might crack in the freezer.)

Chilly Chilled Trifle

This English cake-cream-and-fruit dessert is great for parties. It's so good, it could be the reason for the party.

Ingredients

- 4 cups milk
- 1/3 cup cornstarch
- 1 cup sugar
- 1/2 teaspoon salt
- 3 eggs
- 1 teaspoon vanilla extract
- 2 pounds fresh ripe berries, peaches, kiwi, banana, and/or mango, peeled, hulled, and sliced (I used raspberries and kiwi for this one.)
- 1 loaf of pound cake (page 78), or a store-bought angel food or sponge cake, cut into 1-inch cubes
- about 1/2 cup apple or white grape juice

Makes: around 12 servings

Equipment

- measuring cups and spoons • heavy-bottomed saucepot—not aluminum or your pastry cream will turn gray • mixing bowl • whisk • ladle • large glass serving bowl • plastic wrap

You can prepare this dessert in less than half an hour, but it must chill overnight for the best flavor.

1. Heat the milk in the saucepot on medium heat until it steams but doesn't bubble. Meanwhile, whisk the cornstarch, sugar, salt, and eggs together in the mixing bowl until smooth.

2. Ladle a spoonful of hot milk into the egg mixture, and whisk it up. (This is called tempering the eggs.) Then pour the tempered eggs into the pot of milk. Cook, whisking gently the whole time, 5 to 10 minutes, until the mixture thickens and just starts to bubble. You've just made pastry cream! Now remove it from the heat and whisk in the vanilla extract.

3. Okay, now the fun part. Save the prettiest pieces of fruit for the top. Then layer pastry cream, fruit, and cake in the serving bowl, until you use it all up. Every time you make a layer of cake, sprinkle a few tablespoons of juice on it.

4. Finish layering with the last of the pastry cream, and use the fruit you saved in step 3 to decorate the top. Cover the bowl with plastic wrap—let it rest on top of the trifle, or the pastry cream will develop a skin. Refrigerate overnight, or at least 5 hours, before serving.

Flamenco **Flan**

Clap your hands. Stomp your feet. This Spanish caramel custard deserves its own dance. Olé!

Ingredients

- 1 cup sugar
- ¼ cup water
- 12 ounces evaporated milk (not sweetened condensed milk)
- 2 whole eggs
- 4 egg yolks (See page 30 for tips on separating eggs.)
- ⅔ cup sugar
- 2 teaspoons vanilla extract

Makes: 6 servings

If you don't have evaporated milk or can't find your can opener, you can substitute 1½ cups of regular milk in the recipe. The flan's texture will be less creamy, but it will still taste great.

Equipment

- measuring cups and spoons • can opener • two 1-quart sauce-pots with lids • whisk • 6 individual-size baking dishes, or 1 large baking dish, 8 to 10 inches in diameter • adult helper • heat-proof rubber spatula • mixing bowl • baking dish or roasting pan big enough to hold your other baking dishes • ladle • oven mitts • plastic wrap • table knife • serving plates

You'll need 20 minutes to prepare the flan, and 40 to 45 for baking. (Say it flahn. It rhymes with John.) It should chill overnight for the best texture.

1 Preheat the oven to 350°F. Whisk 1 cup of sugar with the water in the saucepot until it's evenly moist, like damp sand. Put it over medium-low heat, with the lid on, for 3 minutes. Take the lid off, but DON'T STIR. Cook the sugar another 3 to 5 minutes, until it has melted and turned amber. You have just caramelized sugar!

continued on next page

2 Pour the caramelized sugar into the baking dishes. Careful—it's super hot. Have your helper hold the pot while you scrape the sugar out with a rubber spatula. (For a tip on how to clean this pot, see page 31.)

3 Heat the evaporated milk in the second saucepot until the milk is steaming, but not bubbling. Meanwhile, whisk the eggs, yolks, sugar, and vanilla extract together in the mixing bowl.

4 Add a little hot milk to the egg mixture to temper it, and then pour the eggs into the milk. Whisk gently to combine the custard—you don't want it to get frothy. Ladle the custard into the caramel-coated baking dishes.

5 Put the baking dishes in the bigger dish or pan. Use an oven mitt to pull the middle oven rack out halfway, and put the dishes-in-

Separating Eggs

You will need as many eggs as your recipe calls for, plus two small bowls.

Grab an egg. Carefully crack it over one of the bowls and open it up so the two eggshell halves are little cups. Some of egg white (the clear goop) will fall into the bowl.

Gently pass the egg yolk (the yellow part) from one half of the shell to the other. Let the white ooze out into the bowl.

After a few passes, you'll have all the white in the bowl below your hands, and the yolk in the shell. Pour the yolk into the second bowl. Discard the shell.

Variations

Substitute coconut milk for part of the evaporated milk. The flan looks the same, but the taste is a delicious surprise.

Or, add 1 tablespoon orange zest to the milk while it heats. Strain the custard when you pour it into the baking dish to remove the zest. The yummy citrus flavor stays with the dessert.

Or, maybe you want a different kind of zest? Add 1 tablespoon instant espresso powder to the evaporated milk. If you're sensitive to caffeine, skip this variation!

a-dish on it. Pour hot water in the bigger dish, up to the surface level of the custard. Close the oven, and bake 40 to 45 minutes (45 to 50 for a large flan).

6   Have your adult helper use oven mitts to pull the double-dish setup out of the oven. The flan will still be jiggly. Let it sit in the hot water for another 15 to 20 minutes, and then take it out of the water (use oven mitts if the dish is still hot). Cover the flan with plastic wrap and put it in the fridge.

7   Chill your flan overnight in the refrigerator, or for at least 4 hours. Run the knife between the baking dish and the sides of the flan. Put the serving plate upside-down on top of the baking dish, and flip everything over. If your flan doesn't slide onto the plate, use the tip of your knife to gently push the flan away from the side of the dish.

Pot Cleaning Tip

Check out the pot that you used to caramelize sugar for the recipe. That sugar is stuck in there like cement, huh? Before you throw away the pot, try this easy trick:

Fill the pot half full of water. Put it on the stove and turn the burner up to high. Bring the water to a boil. Boil for 3 minutes, and then turn the stove off. Let the pot and water cool down a bit so you don't risk sloshing boiling water on yourself. Then use oven mitts to grab the pot and dump out the water. Your pot will be sparkling clean.

Ice Cream Spumoni

A slice of this Italian dessert looks like a rainbow on your plate. It tastes like the treasure at the end of the rainbow.

Equipment

• rubber spatula • 2½ quart plastic bowl • measuring cups and spoons • mixing bowl • electric mixer • serving plate • kitchen towel

Ingredients

- 1 quart strawberry ice cream
- ½ cup mini chocolate chips
- 1 quart pistachio ice cream (or your favorite flavor)
- 1 cup maraschino cherries, cut in half
- 1 cup (8 ounces) whipping cream
- 2 tablespoons sugar
- 1 tablespoon cocoa powder
- ½ teaspoon vanilla extract
- ⅓ cup pistachios or slivered almonds

Makes: 8 to 10 slices

Because the ice cream gets refrozen a couple of times, this dessert requires a little more than 1½ hours to prepare. Don't worry—you'll only be working for 20 to 30 minutes.

1 Take the strawberry ice cream out of the freezer for 5 to 10 minutes, until it's soft but not melting. Use the rubber spatula to spread it over the bottom and sides of the bowl. (If the ice cream won't stay put, return it to the freezer for a few minutes.) Sprinkle the mini chocolate chips all over the ice cream. Put the bowl back in the freezer for 30 minutes.

2 Soften the pistachio ice cream and spread it over the strawberry layer. Press cherries into it, and then put the whole thing back in the freezer.

3 Whip the cream with the sugar, cocoa powder, and vanilla extract until it forms soft peaks. Fold the nuts into the whipped cream. Put this mixture in the bowl on top of all the ice cream, and smooth the top. Freeze for at least 1 hour.

4 Flip the frozen bowl over onto a serving plate. Run hot water over a towel, and then wring it out. Put the hot towel on the bowl to melt the outer layer of ice cream. Press on the sides of the bowl to loosen the ice cream. After you hear the spumoni fall on the plate, lift the bowl away. Garnish with pistachios. Slice and serve.

Strawberry-Rhubarb Hot-Yum Sundae

Granola adds a delicious, nutritious crunch to this simple dessert. For a lower-fat treat, substitute yogurt for the ice cream.

Equipment

• measuring cups • ice cream scoop or spoon • serving dish

Ingredients

• 2 or 3 scoops vanilla ice cream
• about ½ cup strawberry-rhubarb compote, warm (recipe below)
• 2 or 3 handfuls granola

Makes: 1 sundae per recipe

The topping takes an hour to cook. If you make it ahead of time, then you only need a minute or two to create the sundae.

1 Layer the ice cream, compote, and granola in a bowl so that it looks pretty. Dig in!

Strawberry-Rhubarb Compote

Makes: about 4 cups

Ingredients

• 2 stalks rhubarb, peeled and chopped (about 2 cups)
• 1 pound strawberries, hulled and sliced
• ½ to 1 cup sugar
• ½ teaspoon cinnamon

Equipment

• measuring cups and spoons
• saucepot
• wooden spoon

1 Put all the ingredients in the saucepot and cook on low heat, stirring occasionally, for 1 hour. Store leftover compote in a sealed container in the fridge for up to 2 weeks.

Green Tea and Honeydew Granita

Japanese flavors inspired me to make the recipe for this sweet frozen treat. Make it on a hot day.

Ingredients

- ½ honeydew melon, seeded, peeled, and chopped
- 2 individual-serving size bags green tea
- 2 cups boiling water
- ⅓ to ½ cup sugar

Makes: 8 to 10 servings

Equipment

- blender or food processor • measuring cups • 2-quart plastic storage container with lid • fork

This recipe only takes 15 minute to prep, but you'll need almost 5 hours to freeze it.

1 Purée the honeydew in the blender. You should end up with 2 or 3 cups.

2 Put the tea bags in a large heat-proof measuring cup. Pour 2 cups of boiling water over them. Let the tea steep for 3 to 5 minutes—no longer or it will taste bitter—and then remove the tea bags.

3 Add the sugar to the hot tea and stir until it's dissolved. Combine the melon purée and the tea in the storage container.

4 Put the mixture in the freezer. Every hour, take it out and stir it with a fork. Stab around the edges of the container to break up the ice crystals. After 4 or 5 hours, you'll have a fluffy, frozen treat that's ready to eat. I dressed it up with a fortune cookie for the photo.

Indian Rice Pudding

This incredible dessert is a great treat to soothe your taste buds after a spicy meal.

Equipment

- measuring cups and spoons • heavy-bottomed 2-quart saucepot • wooden spoon • storage container with lid • knife (optional) • grater (optional)

Ingredients

- ½ cup long-grained rice, such as basmati
- 5 cups milk
- 3 cardamom pods (Find these in the spice aisle.)
- ¼ cup sugar
- ¼ cup golden raisins
- ¼ cup shelled pistachios or slivered almonds
- 1 tablespoon rosewater (Optional—look for it in the spice aisle or at an Indian market.)
- 1 apple, cored and grated (Optional—this isn't traditional, but they add apple at my fave Indian restaurant, and I love it.)

Makes: 6 to 8 servings

You'll only be actually working for about 15 minutes, but you'll need almost 2 hours to prepare this recipe. Plus a few hours to chill it.

1. Bring the rice, milk, and cardamom pods to a boil. Reduce the heat to low, and simmer 1½ hours, stirring occasionally, until thickened. The pudding will thicken more when it cools, so kind of soupy is okay at this stage.

2. If you want, you can take the cardamom pods out of the pudding now. (I like the surprise of biting into a cardamom pod, so I leave them in.) Add the sugar, raisins, and nuts. Stir to combine.

3. Refrigerate the pudding a few hours until it's chilled. Just before serving, stir in the rosewater and grated apple. Enjoy!

Munchies

Crunch and munch on these half-dozen recipes for chewy cookies and bars.

Lemon Squares

My friend Rebekah and I loved to make lemon squares after school. Warning: They must cool before you cut them, and the wait can be torture.

Equipment

- measuring cups and spoons • food processor • 9 x 13-inch baking dish, greased • fork • mixing bowl • whisk • oven mitts • sifter

Ingredients

- 2 cups flour
- ½ cup powdered sugar, plus extra for garnish
- 2 sticks (1 cup) cold butter, cut into chunks
- 4 eggs
- 2 cups sugar
- ¼ cup flour
- ½ teaspoon baking powder
- ¼ teaspoon salt
- 1 tablespoon lemon zest
- ½ cup lemon juice (from 2 or 3 lemons)

Makes: 15 squares of lemony goodness

Don't rush these lemon squares. You'll need about a half-hour to prepare them, plus almost an hour to cook, and another half-hour for cooling.

1 Preheat the oven to 350°F. Put the 2 cups of flour, powdered sugar, and butter in the food processor. Turn it on and watch until the mixture forms a ball of dough. Turn it off.

2 Press the dough into the baking dish with your hands and prick it all over with a fork. Bake 20 minutes. Use oven mitts to remove the baking dish from the oven.

continued on next page

3 While the crust is baking, make the lemon filling. Break the eggs into the mixing bowl and whisk until your arm gets tired. Add the sugar, ¼ cup flour, baking powder, and salt. Whisk until all the lumps dissolve. Whisk in the zest and juice until evenly blended.

4 Pour the lemon mixture over the baked crust. Bake another 25 to 30 minutes, until slightly brown at the edges. Use oven mitts to remove the dessert from the oven. Now the hard part: wait for it to cool before cutting it into squares. Sift powdered sugar on top.

Zesting a Lemon

First, make sure you rinse the lemon under hot water to remove any wax from the peel. Then, pull the lemon across the small holes of a box grater or a microplane grater. The sharp edge will cut off tiny pieces of the colored part of the peel,

Because of the custardy top layer, leftover lemon squares should be stored in a sealed container in the refrigerator. They'll stay fresh for several days. (As if they can go that long without being eaten...)

Chocolate-Mint Cookies

Chocolate is an awesome force of nature. I am entrusting you with a powerful recipe. Use it wisely—with a glass of cold milk.

Equipment

• measuring cups and spoons • 2 mixing bowls • electric mixer or fork and muscles • spoon • 2 greased cookie sheets • oven mitts • metal spatula • wire cooling rack

Ingredients

- 1 stick (½ cup) butter, softened
- ¾ cup (packed) brown sugar
- 1 egg
- ¾ teaspoon peppermint extract
- ¾ cup all-purpose flour
- ¾ cup cocoa powder
- ½ teaspoon baking soda
- ¼ teaspoon salt
- ¾ cup chocolate chips

Makes: 24 cookies

Don't do mint? Substitute vanilla extract for the peppermint extract.

This recipe takes about 20 minutes to prepare and 8 to 10 minutes to bake.

1 Preheat oven to 375°F. Cream the butter and brown sugar in a mixing bowl until fluffy. Add the egg and peppermint extract, and beat until combined.

2 Stir the flour, cocoa powder, baking soda, and salt together in the second bowl. Mash any lumps with your fingers. Add this dry stuff to the wet mixture. Mix well.

3 Add the chips. Scrape the bottom of the bowl to make sure everything is evenly blended.

4 Put spoonfuls of dough a couple inches apart on the cookie sheets. Bake 8 to 10 minutes.

5 Use oven mitts to remove the cookie sheets from the oven. Use the metal spatula to transfer the hot cookies to a wire cooling rack.

The Sweetest Snowballs

I've seen these called Mexican, Danish, or Greek Wedding Cookies. Add nuts and they're called Russian Tea Cookies. Everyone wants to take credit for these tasty morsels!

Ingredients

- 2 sticks (1 cup) butter, softened
- ½ cup powdered sugar, plus another ½ cup for "snow"
- 1 teaspoon vanilla extract
- 2 cups flour
- ¼ teaspoon salt
- ½ teaspoon ground anise (optional)
- ½ cup chopped pecans (optional)

Makes: about 40 little cookies

Equipment

- measuring cups and spoons • mixing bowl • electric mixer • spoon • greased cookie sheet • oven mitts • metal spatula • lunch-sized paper bag

These cookies can be ready in about 45 minutes, including the baking time.

1 Preheat the oven to 350°F. Cream the butter and sugar in the mixing bowl until fluffy. Add the vanilla extract and beat until combined. Add the flour, salt, and anise and beat until you have dough. If you're using nuts, mix them in now, until they're evenly distributed.

2 Use your clean hands to roll small spoonfuls of dough into balls. Place them on the baking sheet. The cookies spread out in the oven, so make the balls tinier than you want the finished cookies to be.

3 Bake 20 to 25 minutes (less for really tiny cookies) until slightly brown at the edges and dry on top. Use oven mitts to remove the cookie sheet from the oven.

4 Put about ½ cup of powdered sugar in the paper bag. Transfer the warm cookies to the bag and shake it up. Be gentle—the goal is to have sugar-coated cookies, not sugar mixed with crumbs.

Six-Layer Bars

Graham cracker, milk, chocolate, butterscotch, pecan, and coconut...I can't think of six layers of flavors I'd rather eat all at once!

Equipment

- measuring cups and spoons • mixing bowl • greased 9 x 13-inch baking dish • can opener • rubber spatula • oven mitts

Ingredients

- 1¾ cups graham cracker crumbs
- ½ teaspoon cinnamon
- 1 stick (½ cup) butter, melted
- 14-ounce can of sweetened condensed milk (not evaporated milk)
- 1 cup chocolate chips
- 1 cup butterscotch chips
- 1 cup chopped pecans
- 1½ cups coconut flakes

Makes: 18 bars

These treats take about 15 minutes to put together and 25 to 30 minutes to bake.

1 Preheat the oven to 350°F. Combine the graham cracker crumbs, cinnamon, and melted butter in the mixing bowl. Use your clean hands to mix until evenly moistened, like damp sand. Press the crumb mixture into the baking dish.

2 Pour the sweetened condensed milk over the crumb crust. Use the rubber spatula to get every last bit out of the can. (Don't use your finger! I once cut myself badly that way.)

3 Sprinkle the chips, nuts, and coconut over the condensed milk. Use the spatula to gently press the goodies into the goop. (This time you can use your hands if you want, but be prepared to lick off a big mess.)

4 Bake 25 to 30 minutes. Let the food cool before you cut it into squares. Enjoy.

Chocolate Cherry Cheesecake Brownies

You read it right. Chocolate cherry cheesecake brownies. Need I say more?

Ingredients

- 1½ sticks (¾ cup) butter
- 4 squares (4 ounces) unsweetened baking chocolate
- 2½ cups sugar, divided
- 3 eggs
- 1½ cup flour
- ¼ teaspoon salt
- 8-ounce package cream cheese, softened to room temperature
- 1 teaspoon vanilla extract
- 14-ounce can of tart red cherries packed in juice, drained

Makes: 15 chewy brownies

Equipment

- measuring cups and spoons • 2 mixing bowls (microwave safe—not metal) • wooden spoon • 9 x 13-inch baking dish, greased • rubber spatula • can opener • oven mitts

It takes about 20 minutes to make these brownies and 35 to 40 minutes to bake them.

1. Preheat the oven to 350°F. Microwave the butter and chocolate together in a bowl for 2 minutes on high. Then stir until the chocolate is melted.

2. Add 2 cups of sugar and the eggs to the heated chocolate and butter. Stir until well combined. Then stir in the flour and salt.

3. In the other bowl, combine the cream cheese, ½ cup of sugar, and the vanilla extract. You'll have to put some muscle into stirring this mixture until it's well-blended. Small cream cheese lumps are no big deal.

4. Spread the chocolate mixture in the baking dish. Dollop spoonfuls of the cream cheese mixture on top of the chocolate. Add the drained cherries, right on top. Swirl the rubber spatula through both mixtures to get a marbleized look.

5. Bake 35 to 40 minutes. Use oven mitts to remove the baking dish from the oven. Let the brownies cool before you cut them into, well, brownies.

Raspberry Triangles

If you've never had homemade fruit bars, your life is about to change. You won't settle for the store-bought kind again.

Ingredients

- 1½ cups flour
- 1 cup (packed) brown sugar
- 1 teaspoon salt
- ½ teaspoon baking powder
- 1½ sticks (¾ cup) cold butter, cut into chunks
- 1 cup rolled oats (old-fashioned or quick—not instant)
- 1 cup sweetened shredded coconut (optional), or
- ½ cup chopped walnuts (optional)
- 10-ounce jar raspberry jam (I think the sugar-free, all-fruit kind has the most deliciously intense flavor.)

Makes: 15 triangles

Equipment

- measuring cups and spoons • food processor • mixing bowl • 9 x 13-inch baking dish, greased • rubber spatula • oven mitts • table knife

These bars take about 20 minutes to put together and 35 to 40 minutes to bake.

1 Preheat the oven to 375°F. Put the flour, brown sugar, salt, and baking powder in the food processor, and pulse to combine. Add the butter and process while you count to 20. (The mixture shouldn't have any chunks of butter.)

2 Dump the flour mixture into a mixing bowl. Add the oats, and coconut or walnuts, and stir to combine. Press about ¾ of the mixture into the bottom of the baking dish. Really mash it hard with clean hands.

3 Spread the raspberry jam in an even layer on top of the crust. Sprinkle the rest of the crumb mixture on top of the jam.

4 Bake 35 to 40 minutes, until the top is browned. Use oven mitts to remove the baking dish from the oven. Let the dessert cool to room temperature before cutting into triangles. Dig in!

Pie in the Sky

You aren't dreaming. These recipes for pies—and a few pie-ish goodies—are for real.

Chocolate Meringue Pie

If I had to choose my favorite dessert, this would be it. The rich chocolate, airy meringue, and flaky pastry complement each other perfectly.

Equipment

- measuring cups and spoons • clean, flat work surface • rolling pin • 9-inch pie plate • microwave-safe bowl (not metal) • mixing bowl • rubber spatula • oven mitts • paper towel • electric mixer

Ingredients

- a little bit of flour
- half recipe Primo Piecrust (See page 58.)
- two 4-ounce semisweet or bittersweet chocolate bars (I like to use one of each.)
- ½ stick (¼ cup) butter
- 4 eggs, separated (See page 30.)
- ½ cup milk
- 1 teaspoon vanilla extract
- splash of vinegar
- ¼ cup sugar

Makes: 10 to 12 servings—This pie is ultra-rich, so cut small slices.

This pie takes about 45 minutes prep time, 45 minutes baking time, and 15 minutes cooling time. It's totally worth it!

1. Preheat the oven to 350°F. Make the piecrust following the instructions on pages 58-59.

2. Break the chocolate bars into little pieces. Microwave the chocolate and butter in the microwave-safe bowl for 30 to 60 seconds, until the butter is melted. Stir until the chocolate is melted.

3. Combine the egg yolks, milk, and vanilla extract in the mixing bowl. Stir until well blended. Gradually add the chocolate mixture to the milk mixture. Stir until smooth and evenly chocolaty. Scrape the chocolate filling into the piecrust, and bake 35 minutes. Use oven mitts to remove the pie plate from the oven.

4. While the pie bakes, wash and dry your mixing bowl. Then wipe the inside with a vinegary paper towel. (The bowl should still look dry. This is the trick for whipping egg whites.) Pour the egg whites into the clean bowl. Gradually add the sugar to the egg whites as you whip on high speed. As soon as the meringue looks glossy bright white, stop mixing.

continued on next page

5 Pile the meringue on top of the baked chocolate pie. Spread it so that it touches the crust all the way around. (That keeps the meringue from shrinking as it cooks.) Make pretty curlicues by pulling the spatula up from the meringue.

6 Bake another 7 to 10 minutes, until the meringue is slightly browned. Use oven mitts to remove the meringued pie from the oven. Let the pie cool before serving. Don't worry—the meringue isn't going anywhere without you.

. . . .

Meringue Topping

If you want to add a meringue topping to a pie, use this recipe.

Ingredients

- Baked pie of your choice (See Key Lime Pie on page 60.)
- 4 egg whites (See page 30 for tips on separating eggs.)
- ¼ cup sugar

Equipment

- Mixing bowl
- Electric mixer
- Rubber spatula

1 Put the egg whites in your clean mixing bowl. Beat on medium speed until they're foamy. Turn your mixer up to high speed as you do the next step.

2 Gradually add the sugar to the whites as you beat. The egg whites will change from foamy

Want Perfectly Fluffy Egg Whites?

Although it's easiest to separate eggs when they're cold, the egg whites whip up better at room temperature. Also, egg whites won't whip if there is even a tiny smidge of grease in the bowl. So, wash the mixing bowl in hot water, then dry it well. (The warm bowl will help take the chill off of the egg whites.)

Next, dampen a paper towel with white vinegar, and use it to rub the inside of the bowl. This will remove any trace of grease. De-grease your beaters with the vinegary paper towel, too. Now you're all set for foolproof whipping!

P.S. Don't get confused and use this tip when you're whipping cream—the bowl should be cold for that.

to frothy to bubble-bathy to shaving-creamy, which is just the right texture for meringue. Stop mixing as soon as the meringue looks glossy bright white. (If you over-beat, the meringue won't look as beautiful when you swirl it atop the pie in step 3, but it will still taste great.)

3 Use the spatula to pile the meringue on top of your baked pie. Spread it so that it touches the crust all the way around. (That keeps the meringue from shrinking as it cooks.) Make pretty curlicues by pulling the spatula up from the meringue.

4 Put the pie in the oven and bake 7 to 10 minutes, until the meringue is slightly browned. Use oven mitts to remove the pie from the oven. Let the pie cool before serving.

Primo Piecrust

The key to making piecrust dough that's easy to work with and bakes up crisp and flaky is to keep the ingredients cold. After you measure, stick everything in the freezer for a couple minutes.

Makes: two 9-inch single-crust pies, or one 9-inch double-crust pie

Ingredients

- 2¼ cups all-purpose flour
- ¼ teaspoon salt
- ¼ teaspoon baking powder
- 1¾ sticks (7 ounces) butter, cut into 1-inch chunks
- ⅓ cup super-cold water
- 1 teaspoon vinegar

Equipment

- measuring cups and spoons
- food processor or pastry blender and wooden spoon
- chilled mixing bowl
- plastic wrap
- pastry board
- rolling pin
- greased pie plate (I like glass ones best.)
- kitchen shears or paring knife

Your piecrust will be ready for use in a little more than half an hour.

1 **Food Processor Method:** Put the chilled flour, salt, and baking powder in the bowl of the food processor fitted with the blade attachment. Pulse three times to combine. Add the butter, and pulse five times. You should be able to see little pieces of butter, but none of them should be bigger than a raisin. See photo A. Combine the water and vinegar, and add them to the flour mixture. Pulse five more times. Unplug the food processor, and dump the crumbly dough into the mixing bowl.

Hand Method: Combine the chilled flour, salt, and baking powder in the mixing bowl. Cut in the butter with the pastry blender. See photo B. You should be able to see little pieces of butter, but none of them should be bigger than a raisin. Combine the water and vinegar, and add them to the flour mixture. Stir lightly until the water is evenly distributed.

2 Use your hands to squeeze the dough, kneading just until it comes together in a ball. Divide the dough in half and form each half into a disk.

A.

B.

C.

D.

E.

3 Wrap the disks in plastic wrap and put them in the fridge for at least 15 minutes. (If you only need one of the disks today, double wrap the other one and put it in the freezer. The next time you make a pie, just let this dough thaw until you can roll it out.)

4 Sprinkle a little bit of flour on your pastry board and rub some on the rolling pin. Unwrap a chilled dough disk and put it on the board. Roll out the piecrust by starting in the middle and pushing the rolling pin down and away from you to the edge of the dough. Give the dough a quarter turn, and repeat the rolling. Keep turning and rolling until the dough is about ¼ inch thick. See photo C. You may need to sprinkle some more flour if the dough sticks to the board or rolling pin. If the dough becomes difficult to work with as you roll it out, put it in the fridge for a while.

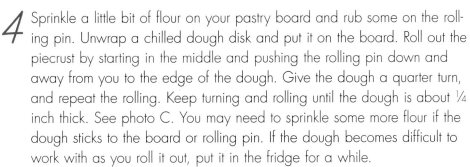
F.

5 To transfer the dough to the pie plate, roll it loosely around the rolling pin, move it over the pie plate, and unroll it into the plate. See photos D and E. It's important not to stretch the dough up the sides of the plate, or the dough will shrink when it bakes. Just ease it in.

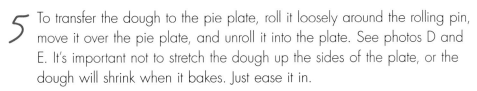

6 Use the kitchen shears or paring knife to trim the crust to about ½ inch from the lip of the pie plate. See photo F. Make a ruffled edge by crimping the dough with two fingers and a thumb. See photo G. Your piecrust is ready for filling!

G.

Key Lime Pie

Key limes grow in the Florida Keys. Can't find them? Try Persian limes. Or buy bottled Key lime juice.

Ingredients

- 12 graham crackers
- 2 tablespoons sugar
- ¾ stick (6 tablespoons) butter, melted
- 14-ounce can of sweetened condensed milk
- 3 egg yolks (See page 30 for tips on separating eggs.)
- ½ cup lime juice (from about 9 Key limes or 3 Persian limes)
- 1 tablespoon lime zest

Makes: 6 to 8 servings

A Key lime (the small yellow one) and a Persian lime (the big green one).

Equipment

- large plastic storage bag • rolling pin • measuring cups and spoons • 2 mixing bowls • 9-inch pie plate • can opener • rubber spatula • whisk • oven mitts

You can prepare this recipe in 20 minutes or less, but you'll need more than 2 hours for baking and chilling.

1 Preheat the oven to 350°F. Put the graham crackers in the bag, but don't seal it all the way. (You don't want the bag to burst as you do the next step.) Use the rolling pin to smash the crackers to smithereens. (By smithereens, of course, I mean fine crumbs.)

2 Combine the crumbs, sugar, and melted butter in a mixing bowl. Use your clean hands to mix it together until evenly blended. Press the crumb mixture into the pie plate to make a crust.

3 Use a rubber spatula to scrape the condensed milk out of the can and into the other mixing bowl. Whisk in the egg yolks. Add the lime juice. Whisk some more. At first, the juice will thin the mixture, but then the acid from the limes causes the protein in the milk and eggs to thicken.

4 Fold the lime zest into the filling, and pour it all into the graham cracker crust. Bake 15 minutes. (The filling will still be wobbly when you take it out of the oven.) Let the pie rest at room temperature for 10 minutes. Then refrigerate it for least 2 hours.

5 Traditionally, Key Lime Pie is served with a meringue topping like the one on page 56. I like it with homemade whipped cream. (See page 22.)

Blackberry Cobbler

This is one of those desserts that people go crazy over. They have no idea how easy it is to make. Shhh...why ruin it for them?

Ingredients

- 3 to 4 pints fresh-picked wild blackberries, washed and picked over (You can use two 12-ounce bags of frozen berries instead.)
- 1 to 2 cups sugar (Use the greater amount for wild berries only.)
- ¼ cup cornstarch
- pinch of salt
- 1 teaspoon vanilla extract
- 2 cups flour
- ¼ cup sugar
- 1 tablespoon baking powder
- ½ teaspoon salt
- ½ stick butter (¼ cup), cut into ¼-inch slices
- ¾ cup milk

Makes: 6 to 8 servings

Equipment

- measuring cups and spoons • 2 mixing bowls • wooden spoon • 9 x 13-inch baking dish, greased • oven mitts

This dessert takes about 15 minutes to put together and 35 to 40 minutes to bake.

1 Preheat the oven to 400°F. Combine the berries, sugar, cornstarch, pinch of salt, and vanilla extract in a mixing bowl. Stir until the cornstarch dissolves. Dump the fruit mixture into the baking dish.

2 Stir the flour, ¼ cup sugar, baking powder, and salt together in the second mixing bowl. Work the butter into the flour with your fingers until the texture is crumbly. Add the milk and stir to make shaggy, sticky dough.

3 Drop clumps of dough on top of the fruit in the baking dish. Cobbler got its name because it looks like lumpy, bumpy cobblestone streets—so don't smooth it out. Bake 35 to 40 minutes, until the top is golden brown and the juices are bubbling around the edges. Use oven mitts to remove the baking dish from the oven.

4 Let the cobbler cool while you check the mirror. Do you look like you've suffered to make this special treat for your family? Serve the cobbler with ice cream and a sigh.

Apple Crisp

I love this recipe because I get to use my favorite gadget, an apple peeler/corer/slicer. The crisp is also delicious.

Ingredients

- 5 cups apples, peeled, cored, and sliced (7 or 8 apples. Use firm, tart apples for baking, such as Granny Smiths.)
- 2 tablespoons to ¼ cup brown sugar
- 1 teaspoon cinnamon
- ¾ stick (6 tablespoons) butter, melted
- 1 cup rolled oats (old-fashioned or quick, not instant)
- another ⅓ cup (packed) brown sugar
- ⅓ cup flour
- ¼ teaspoon salt
- ½ cup chopped pecans (optional)

Makes: 8 to 10 servings

Equipment

- measuring cups and spoons • mixing bowl • 9 x 13-inch baking dish, greased • wooden spoon • oven mitts

Once the apples are sliced, it only takes 10 minutes to put this dessert together, followed by 45 to 50 minutes of baking.

1 Preheat the oven to 350°F. Toss the apples, 2 tablespoons to ¼ cup brown sugar, and cinnamon together in the mixing bowl until the apples are evenly coated. Dump the apple mixture into the baking dish. Sprinkle 2 tablespoons of the melted butter on the apples.

2 Combine the rest of the butter, oats, ⅓ cup brown sugar, flour, salt, and nuts. (You can use the same bowl the apples were in—fewer dishes to wash!) Stir the topping until well-blended, and then put it on top of the apples.

3 Bake 45 to 50 minutes, until the top is browned and juice is bubbling at the edges of the dish. Use oven mitts to remove the baking dish from the oven. I like my Apple Crisp with a scoop of ice cream.

Extra-Nutty Pecan Tart

My Aunt Sharon taught me this sophisticated version of chewy, sweet pecan pie. The secret is lots and lots of nuts.

Ingredients

- ½ recipe of Primo Piecrust (page 58)
- a little bit of flour
- 2 cups pecans
- ⅔ cup corn syrup
- ⅔ cup sugar
- 2 eggs
- ¼ stick (2 tablespoons) butter, melted
- 1 teaspoon vanilla extract

Makes: 8 to 10 servings—it's rich, so cut small pieces

Chocolate lover's variation:

Sprinkle 1 cup of chocolate chips on the bottom of the crust before you add the pecans in step 2, and reduce the amount of pecans to 1¼ cup.

Equipment

- clean, flat work surface • rolling pin • measuring cups and spoons • 9-inch tart pan (if you don't have one, use a regular pie plate and increase the baking time by 5 to 10 minutes) • big 4-cup liquid measuring cup • rubber spatula • cookie sheet

This recipe takes about 30 minutes to prep, and 40 to 45 minutes to bake.

1. Preheat the oven to 350°F. Make the piecrust. Press the dough into the corners of the tart pan—remember to not stretch it. Roll your rolling pin over the top edge of the pan to trim off extra dough.

2. Dump the pecans into the crust. Spread them out in an even layer.

3. Measure the corn syrup in the big measuring cup. Add the sugar, eggs, melted butter, and vanilla extract. Stir until well-combined. Pour the sugar mixture over the pecans.

4. Put the empty cookie sheet on a low rack in the oven in case the tart bubbles over. Then put the tart in the oven, on the middle rack. Bake 40 to 45 minutes. Use oven mitts to remove the tart pan from the oven. Serve slightly cooled. Pecan tarts also taste great chilled in the refrigerator.

Strawberry Sticky

Why is it called Strawberry Sticky? Look at your hands when you're finished making it.

Equipment

- measuring cups and spoons • 2 mixing bowls • pastry blender (Optional—I use my hands.) • wooden spoon • clean, flat work surface, sprinkled with a little flour • rolling pin • pizza cutter or paring knife • greased baking dish about the size of this book • oven mitts

Ingredients

- 2 pounds of strawberries, hulled and sliced (Frozen strawberries are fine.)
- ½ cup sugar
- 2 tablespoons cornstarch
- 2 cups flour, plus a little extra for rolling out dough
- ¼ cup sugar
- 1 teaspoon salt
- ½ stick (¼ cup) butter, sliced and chilled
- ½ cup half-and-half (You can use milk if you don't have half-and-half.)

Makes: about 8 servings

This recipe takes about 40 minutes to prepare and 30 to 35 minutes to bake.

1. Preheat the oven to 350°F. Combine the strawberries, ½ cup sugar, and cornstarch in one bowl. Set it aside.

2. Stir the flour, ¼ cup sugar, and salt together in the other bowl. Use your hands or a pastry blender to work the butter into the flour until the mixture looks like coarse crumbs.

3. Add the half-and-half to the flour/butter mixture. Stir it with a wooden spoon until it forms a dough, and then use your hands to work the dough until all the dry crumbs are mixed in.

4. Roll the dough out to about ¼ inch thick. Cut it into 2-inch strips. Fold them in half and mash the ends together into tear-drop shapes.

5. Arrange the dough loops in the baking dish. Stuff the strawberries inside, around, and between the dough. The strawberries will cook down, so pile them higher than the dough, but not on top of it.

6. Bake 30 to 35 minutes, until the fruit is bubbling and the dough is browned. Use oven mitts to remove the baking dish from the oven. Let the dessert cool just a bit before eating.

In-a-Skillet Peach Pie

Does this look cool, or what? Pretend it's the olden days and you're cooking over a fire.

Equipment

- clean flat work surface • rolling pin • 10-inch cast iron skillet (If you don't have one, use a glass pie plate; a light-colored skillet won't work as well.) • mixing bowl • wooden spoon • oven mitts

Ingredients

- 1 full recipe Primo Piecrust (See page 58.)
- 2 pounds peaches, peeled, pitted, and sliced (Frozen peaches work well.)
- 1/4 cup sugar
- 1 tablespoon cornstarch
- 1/4 teaspoon salt
- 1 teaspoon vanilla extract
- 1/4 teaspoon nutmeg
- 1 tablespoon butter, cut into tiny pieces
- another tablespoon of sugar

Makes: about 8 servings

You'll need about half an hour to prepare this recipe, and 50 to 55 minutes for baking.

1. Preheat the oven to 400°F. Read page 58 to learn all of my piecrust tricks. Roll the full recipe of dough into a round 1/8 to 1/4 inch thick. Cracked, uneven edges add to this pie's rustic look. Carefully transfer the giant dough round to the skillet, letting the extra dough drape over the sides.

2. Combine the peaches, sugar, cornstarch, salt, vanilla extract, and nutmeg in a mixing bowl. Stir until the cornstarch is dissolved and the peaches are evenly coated. Dump the peach mixture into the skillet.

3. Scatter the little pieces of butter all over the peaches. Fold the crust over the fruit, leaving the middle open. Sprinkle a tablespoon of sugar over the whole thing.

4. Bake 50 to 55 minutes, until the crust is golden brown and the juice is bubbling. Leave an oven mitt on the skillet's handle after you take it out of the oven to remind yourself that it's hot.

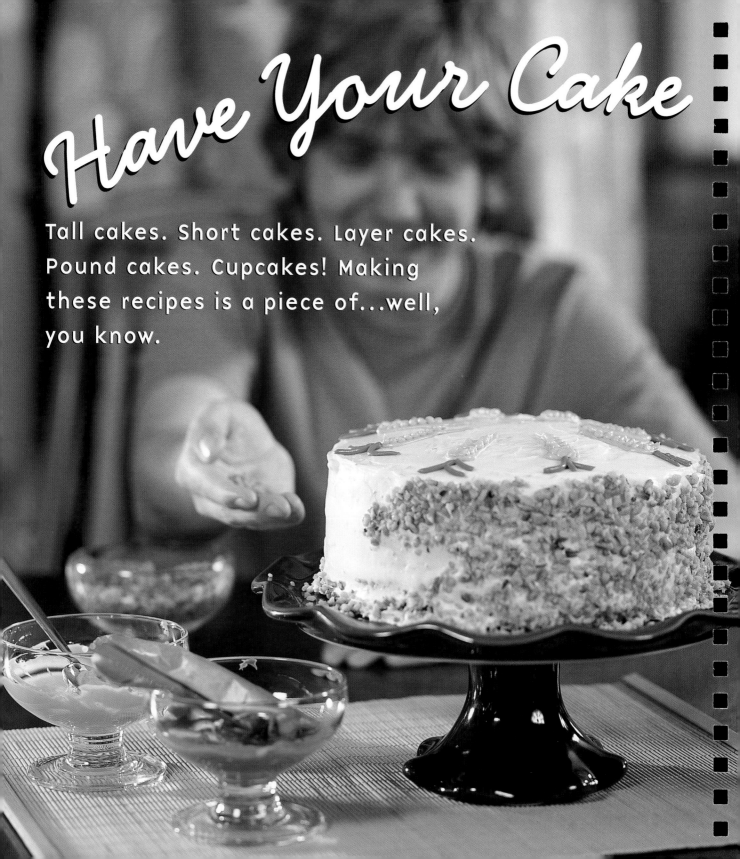

Have Your Cake

Tall cakes. Short cakes. Layer cakes.
Pound cakes. Cupcakes! Making
these recipes is a piece of...well,
you know.

Carrot Cake

Make and share this dessert just once and you'll be remembered forever.

Ingredients

- 2 cups all-purpose flour
- 1 cup sugar
- ½ cup (packed) brown sugar
- 1 teaspoon baking soda
- 1 teaspoon baking powder
- 1 teaspoon salt
- 1 teaspoon cinnamon
- 1 cup cooking oil, such as canola
- 4 eggs
- 4 cups shredded carrots (about 8 carrots)
- 1 cup raisins (optional)
- 1 cup walnuts (optional)
- Classic Cream Cheese frosting (See page 92.)
- extra nuts for decorating (optional)

Makes: 1 triple layer cake
or 1 sheet cake

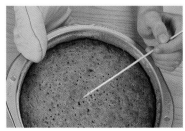
Use a skewer to test for doneness.

Equipment

- measuring cups and spoons • sifter • mixing bowl • electric mixer • rubber spatula • three 9-inch cake pans, greased and floured, or 9 x 13-inch baking dish, greased and floured • skewer, toothpick, or fork • oven mitts • wire cooling racks • pastry bags (See page 82.)

You can make this cake in about half an hour and then bake it for 40 to 45 minutes. Frosting it will take another 20 minutes or so.

1 Preheat the oven to 325°F. Sift the flour into the mixing bowl. Add the sugar, brown sugar, baking soda, baking powder, salt, and cinnamon. Stir to combine.

2 Add the oil and eggs to the flour mixture. Mix on low speed until the flour is moistened. Turn the mixer up to medium and beat while you count to 50.

3 Use the rubber spatula to fold in the carrots, raisins, and nuts. Scrape the bottom of the bowl to make sure everything is evenly blended.

4 Fill your baking dish halfway with batter. Bake 40 to 45 minutes for layer cake, or 50 to 55 minutes for sheet cake, until a skewer stuck in the center comes out with a few sticky crumbs, but no wet batter. Use oven mitts to remove the baking dish from the oven. Let the cake cool on a cooling rack before you frost it. I decorated my cake with chopped walnuts on the sides and icing carrots on top.

continued on next page

Layer Cakes

1 To frost and build a layer cake, start with one layer on a serving plate. (Make sure you begin the process on the plate you want to use to serve your dessert. It's really hard to move a finished cake without messing up the frosting! You can tuck strips of waxed paper under the cake to keep the plate clean, as you see in the photo.) Use an offset spatula to spread a medium layer of frosting on the top so the cake is evenly covered. (You don't want to skimp on this layer.)

2 Stack the second layer on top of the frosted layer. Make sure it's a good stack—line it up right on top of the first cake. Now spread frosting on this cake-top. (Use a medium amount of frosting again.)

3 Add the third layer of cake to the stack. Spread a thin layer of frosting on the whole cake, right down to the serving plate. (This is called the crumb layer. It traps any stray crumbs that might not be so pretty on your finished cake.) Don't worry about how it looks, yet. You should have a little less than half of your frosting left.

4 Put the cake in the freezer for 5 minutes until the crumb layer has hardened and trapped the crumbs.

5 Remove the cake from the freezer and cover the sides with frosting. Then top with the remaining frosting. Take away the waxed paper to reveal a perfectly clean serving plate. You can make swirls or add designs in more icing. Or, maybe you should top this cake with a birthday candle.

Frosting Cakes, Sheet Cakes, and Cupcakes

Use an offset spatula or a table knife to spread a layer of frosting on the whole cake, right down to the serving plate or cupcake paper. Experiment making swirls in the frosting with the spatula. Lick the spatula when you are finished.

Apple Spice Cake

This luscious cake is chock-full of perfectly baked apples. Eat a warm slice of it on a crisp autumn day.

Equipment

- measuring cups and spoons • 2 mixing bowls • small bowl • electric mixer • rubber spatula
- bundt pan, greased and floured • skewer or toothpick • oven mitts • serving plate

Ingredients

- 4 eggs
- 1 stick (½ cup) butter, softened to room temperature
- ¾ cup sugar
- ¾ cup (packed) brown sugar
- ¼ cup cooking oil, such as canola
- 2 teaspoons vanilla extract
- 2 cups all-purpose flour
- 1 teaspoon baking powder
- 1 teaspoon baking soda
- 1 teaspoon salt
- 1 teaspoon cinnamon
- ½ teaspoon nutmeg
- ¼ teaspoon cloves
- 4 or 5 tart apples, peeled, cored, and diced (4 cups)
- ½ cup chopped pecans (optional)
- ½ cup golden raisins (optional)
- Lemon Glaze (See page 93.)

Makes: 1 bundt cake

This dessert takes about half an hour to prepare, plus 35 to 40 minutes of baking.

1 Preheat the oven to 350°F. Separate the eggs. Beat the whites in a mixing bowl. (See page 56 for egg white tips.) Save the yolks. Set the whites aside.

2 In the other mixing bowl, cream the butter, sugar, and brown sugar. Add the oil, egg yolks, and vanilla extract. Beat until smooth.

3 Add the flour, baking powder, baking soda, salt, and spices to the butter mixture. Mix on low until the flour is moistened. Then turn the mixer up to medium and beat while you count to 50.

4 Use a rubber spatula to fold the egg whites into the batter. Make sure everything is well blended. Fold in the apples, nuts, and raisins.

5 Scrape the batter into the bundt pan. Bake 35 to 40 minutes, until a skewer stuck in the center comes out with a few moist crumbs, but no wet batter. Use oven mitts to remove the baking pan from the oven.

6 Let the cake rest a few minutes. Then flip it over onto the serving plate. Remove the pan. Drizzle lemon glaze on the cake while it's warm.

Perfect Pound Cake

Talk about a simple recipe! This moist, filling cake is made of a pound each of butter, sugar, eggs, and flour.

Equipment

- measuring cups and spoons • 2 mixing bowls • electric mixer • rubber spatula
- 2 loaf pans, greased and floured (or you could use three 9-inch cake pans or 1 bundt pan) • skewer or toothpick • oven mitts • table knife • wire cooling rack

Ingredients

- 4 sticks (2 cups/1 pound) butter, softened to room temperature
- 2 cups sugar
- 1 tablespoon vanilla extract
- 6 eggs
- 3 cups cake flour, sifted
- ½ teaspoon salt
- 2 teaspoons baking powder

Makes: 2 loaves (about 8 servings per loaf)

Want a lemon pound cake? Add 1 tablespoon of lemon zest to the batter.

This cake takes about 20 minutes to make and 1 hour to bake.

1. Preheat the oven to 350°F. Cream the butter and sugar in a mixing bowl until fluffy. Add the vanilla extract. Add the eggs one at a time, beating for 30 seconds after each addition.

2. In a separate bowl, combine the sifted flour, salt, and baking powder. Stir it up. Add the flour mixture to the egg mixture about 1 cup at a time, beating for 30 seconds between additions. Scrape the bottom of the bowl with a rubber spatula to make sure everything's mixed together.

3. Divide the batter between the prepared pans. Smooth the tops with your rubber spatula. Bake 60 to 65 minutes until a toothpick stuck in the center comes out with only a few crumbs stuck to it. Use oven mitts to remove the baking pans from the oven.

4. Run a knife between the sides of the pans and the cakes, and then flip them onto a cooling rack. If you want to add the Lemon Glaze from page 93, pour it on while the cakes are warm.

5. I like to eat one loaf while it's warm, and put the other one in the freezer for later—or to use for another dessert recipe. (See pages 80 and 26.) To freeze a cake, let it cool, wrap it in plastic wrap, stick it in a freezer bag, and then freeze it for up to 4 months.

Teeny, Tiny, Tasty Cakes

The only time it's a good idea to eat an entire cake is when you have these bite-sized beauties in front of you. These French treats are called petits fours.

. . . .

Equipment

• table knife • cutting board • small rubber spatula • pastry brush • measuring cups and spoons • mixing bowl • whisk • spoon • liquid measuring cups • waxed paper • wire rack • pastry bags (See page 82.)

. . . .

Ingredients
• 1 loaf Perfect Pound Cake (See page 78.)
• your favorite jam (I like the no-sugar, all-fruit kind.)
• 2 pounds (about 8 cups) powdered sugar
• ¼ cup light corn syrup
• 1 teaspoon vanilla extract
• ½ cup very hot water
• food coloring

Makes: about 36 little cakes

If you start with the extra loaf of Perfect Pound Cake from page 78, you can prepare these treats in about half an hour.

1 Trim the rough top off of the pound cake. Eat the trimmings. Cut the remaining cake horizontally into four even slices. Spread jam on two of the slices, and then top them with the other two to make cake sandwiches. Cut the sandwiches into bite-sized squares. Use a pastry brush to brush the crumbs off the little cakes.

2 Combine the powdered sugar, corn syrup, vanilla extract, and hot water in a mixing bowl. Whisk until all the lumps are gone. This kind of icing is called poured fondant.

continued on next page

3 Divide the fondant among your liquid measuring cups. Make each batch a different color by adding food coloring a drop at a time until you get the shade you want. Cover each one with waxed paper, so that the paper touches the icing. (Fondant dries out very quickly.)

4 Put your wire rack on top of a sheet of waxed paper. Place three or four tiny cakes on the rack. Pour about 2 tablespoons of fondant over each cake, and use the spatula to quickly spread the fondant over the sides as it drips down. Ice the cakes a few at a time until you're ready to switch colors. (If the fondant becomes too stiff to pour, microwave it for 5 to 10 seconds.)

5 Scrape the fondant drippings off the waxed paper back into the cup and cover it again. Ice the rest of the cakes.

6 By now, the fondant that's been sitting around will have cooled off, making it the perfect consistency for drawing decorations on top of your petits fours. Use a pastry bag. Draw whatever you like!

Making and Using a Pastry Bag

I make one bag for each color of icing I need.

What You Need
• Waxed paper • Flat surface • Scissors • Icing

1 Lay one sheet of waxed paper flat on the your work surface. Fold up one bottom corner to create a triangle. Cut along the fold. See photo A.

2 Bring one point from the base (long side) of the triangle toward the other point of the triangle's base. See photo B.

A.

B.

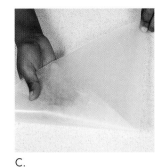

C.

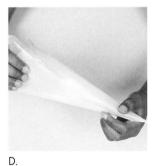

D.

E.

3 Continue pulling the paper so that it begins wrapping around your right hand. See photo C.

4 Shuffle the paper so that the inside piece is tightening while the outer piece continues to wrap into a cone. See photo D.

5 Fold in the pieces at the top of the cone to hold the shape in place. See photo E.

6 Use a spatula or spoon to fill the bag half full with icing. See photo F. Push the icing down into the tip to avoid air pockets.

7 Fold up the end of the bag to seal it. Cut the tip to make a small hole. See photo G.

8 Practice piping on a sheet of waxed paper. See photo H. You'll hold the pointy end of the pastry bag with one hand to guide it and use your other hand to squeeze the end of the bag. Continue folding the bag as it empties.

9 When you are finished practicing, use the same technique on a cake. Throw the pastry bag away after you use and/or eat all of the icing out of it.

F.

G.

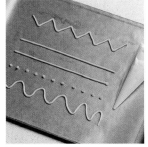

H.

Melt-in-Your-Mouth Chocolate Cupcakes

For super-moist, super-yummy cupcakes, my secret ingredient is zucchini. Yep, those green squash!

Ingredients

- 1 stick (½ cup) butter, softened
- 1¾ cups sugar
- ½ cup cooking oil, such as canola
- 2 eggs
- ½ cup milk
- 1 teaspoon vanilla extract
- 2¼ cups all-purpose flour
- ⅓ cup cocoa powder
- 1 teaspoon baking soda
- 1 teaspoon salt
- ½ teaspoon cinnamon
- 2 cups grated zucchini (1 large or 2 small zucchinis)
- 1 cup chocolate chips (optional)
- icing of your choice (See pages 92-93. I used Raspberry Cream Cheese icing.)
- sprinkles (optional)

Makes: 20 cupcakes

Equipment

- grater • measuring cups and spoons • 2 mixing bowls • electric mixer • sifter • rubber spatula • muffin tins with paper liners • skewer or toothpick • oven mitts

These cupcakes take about half an hour to prepare and 20 to 25 minutes to bake.

1. Preheat the oven to 350° F. Cream the butter and sugar in a mixing bowl until fluffy. Add the oil and eggs. Beat until the mixture is smooth and all the same color.

2. Combine the milk and vanilla extract in a liquid measuring cup. Sift the flour, cocoa powder, baking soda, salt, and cinnamon together into a separate bowl.

3. Add about a third of the flour mixture to the egg mixture. Mix on low until all the flour is wet. Mix in half of the milk. Add some more of the flour mixture, then the rest of the milk, and then the rest of the flour, mixing well between additions.

4. Use your rubber spatula to fold the zucchini and chocolate chips into the batter. Scrape the bottom of the bowl to blend well.

5. Fill each cupcake cup halfway with batter. Bake 20 to 25 minutes, until a skewer stuck in a cupcake center comes out with a few sticky crumbs, but no wet batter. Use oven mitts to remove the cupcake pan from the oven. Let the cupcakes cool before you frost them. (For tips, see page 74.) Go wild with sprinkles.

Upside-Down Cake

This pineapple cake's name comes from the final step—you flip the cake before serving it.

Equipment

- measuring cups and spoons • 10-inch cast iron skillet (If you don't have one, don't use any other kind of skillet. Grab a 2-quart baking dish instead, preferably with handles.)
- heat-proof rubber spatula • 2 mixing bowls • fork • oven mitts • serving plate • helper

Ingredients

- ½ stick (¼ cup) butter
- ½ cup (packed) brown sugar
- 1 cup flour
- ½ cup plain cornmeal (not self-rising)
- ¾ cup sugar
- 1 teaspoon baking powder
- 1 teaspoon baking soda
- 1 teaspoon cinnamon
- 1 cup sour cream
- 2 eggs
- 1 teaspoon vanilla extract
- 1 fresh peeled and cored pineapple, cut into 7 slices
- 4 to 5 maraschino cherries, cut in half
- handful of pecan halves (optional)

Makes: 12 servings

This dessert takes about half an hour to put together and 30 to 35 minutes to bake.

1 Preheat the oven to 350°F. Melt the butter and brown sugar in the skillet over medium heat on the stovetop. Use the rubber spatula to spread the mixture in an even layer over the bottom of the skillet. It will look kind of gloppy and separated, but that's okay. Turn the stove off and let the skillet cool while you make the batter.

2 Use a fork to stir the flour, cornmeal, sugar, baking powder, baking soda, and cinnamon together in a mixing bowl until evenly combined. In another bowl, beat the sour cream, eggs, and vanilla extract together until smooth. Add the egg mixture to the flour mixture, and stir until well-blended.

3 Arrange the pineapple slices, cherries, and pecans in the bottom of the skillet. Scrape the cake batter on top of the fruit. Bake 30 to 35 minutes, until golden brown. Use oven mitts to remove the skillet from the oven.

4 Let the skillet cool until you can comfortably pick it up. (Leave an oven mitt over the handle while it cools to remind yourself not to grab it.) Center the serving plate upside-down over the cake. Ask your helper to flip the skillet and plate over together. Lift the skillet away. Ta-da!

Polka Dot Devil's Cake

Don't let the angelic buttercream frosting fool you—this is a rich, chocolaty devil's food cake.

• •

Equipment

- measuring cups and spoons, including a heat-proof 2-cup liquid measuring cup
- 2 mixing bowls • electric mixer • rubber spatula • sifter • two 9-inch cake pans, greased and floured • oven mitts • skewer or toothpick • wire cooling racks

• •

Ingredients

- 1¼ cup hot water
- ¾ cup cocoa powder
- 1½ sticks (¾ cup) butter, softened
- 1½ cup sugar
- 3 eggs
- 1 teaspoon vanilla extract
- 2 cups all-purpose flour
- 1 teaspoon salt
- 1½ teaspoon baking soda
- frosting of your choice (I used Vanilla Buttercream. See page 92.)
- cinnamon candies (optional)

Makes: 2 cake layers

This cake can be ready in a little more than an hour.

1 Preheat the oven to 350°F. Measure the hot water in the heat-proof cup. Add the cocoa powder, and stir until dissolved.

2 Cream the butter and sugar in a mixing bowl until fluffy. Add the eggs and vanilla extract, and beat until well-combined. Scrape the bottom of the bowl with the rubber spatula to make sure all of the butter is incorporated.

3 Sift the flour, salt, and baking soda together into the second bowl. Add about a third of the flour mixture to the egg mixture, and beat until combined. Then add half of the chocolate mixture, and beat until combined. Go back and forth—flour, chocolate, flour—beating after each addition.

4 Scrape the bottom of the bowl with the rubber spatula, and then beat on medium speed while you count to 50. Fill the cake pans halfway with batter.

5 Bake 30 to 35 minutes, until a skewer stuck in the center comes out with a few moist crumbs but no wet batter. Use oven mitts to remove the baking pan from the oven. Let the cake cool before you frost it. (For tips, see page 74.) I decorated this cake with cinnamon candies.

German's Cake

Sam German, an Englishman, created sweet baking chocolate.
Then a Texan came up with this recipe. It isn't German at all!

Equipment

- measuring cups and spoons • microwave-safe bowl • sifter • rubber spatula
- 2 mixing bowls • electric mixer • three 9-inch cake pans, greased and floured
- oven mitts • skewer or toothpick • table knife • wire cooling racks

Ingredients

- 4-ounce bar German's chocolate (also called sweet baking chocolate)
- ½ cup milk
- 2½ cups cake flour (Use 2¼ cups all-purpose flour if you don't have cake flour.)
- 1½ teaspoon baking soda
- ¼ teaspoon salt
- 2 sticks (1 cup) butter, softened to room temperature
- 1¾ cup sugar
- 4 eggs
- 1 teaspoon vanilla extract
- 1 cup sour cream
- Coconut Pecan frosting (See page 93.)

Makes: about 6 servings

This cake takes about 30 minutes to make, and 25 to 30 minutes to bake.

1. Preheat the oven to 350°F. Microwave the chocolate and milk in the microwave-safe bowl for 1½ minutes on high. Stir until the chocolate is melted. Set aside. Sift the flour, baking soda, and salt together into a different bowl. Set this aside, too.

2. Cream the butter and sugar in a mixing bowl until fluffy. Add the eggs one at a time, beating between each addition. Add half of the flour mixture to the egg mixture. Beat until well combined. Add the vanilla extract and the chocolate mixture. Beat until smooth.

3. Add the rest of the flour mixture. Beat. Add the sour cream. Beat. Scrape the bottom of the bowl with a rubber spatula to incorporate all the ingredients. Beat some more.

4. Divide the batter between the cake pans. Bake 25 to 30 minutes, until a skewer stuck in the center comes out with only a few crumbs, but no sticky batter. Run a knife around the insides of the pans, but wait 10 minutes before you flip the cakes out onto cooling racks.

5. The Coconut Pecan Frosting on page 93 is traditional with this cake. I frosted between the layers and on top of my cake. (For tips, see page 74.) To frost the sides, too, double that recipe.

Frosting Madness and Glaze Goodness

Mix and match these terrific toppings with the cake recipes in this chapter. Each frosting or glaze takes 5 to 10 minutes to prepare.

Classic Cream Cheese

Ingredients

- two 8-ounce packages cream cheese, softened
- 1 stick butter, softened
- 2 cups powdered sugar, sifted
- 1 teaspoon vanilla extract
- zest of 1 orange (Optional, but highly recommended. See page 14 for zesting tips.)

Vanilla Buttercream

Ingredients

- 1½ sticks butter, softened
- 3 cups powdered sugar, sifted
- ¼ cup milk
- 1½ teaspoons vanilla extract

Raspberry Cream Cheese

Ingredients

- 8-ounce package cream cheese, softened
- ½ stick (¼ cup) butter, softened
- ½ cup raspberry jam or fruit spread (The kind without sugar tastes extra-fruity.)
- 2½ cups powdered sugar, sifted

Equipment

- measuring cups and spoons
- sifter
- mixing bowl
- electric mixer

1 To make any one of these recipes, put everything in the bowl. Mix on low until the ingredients are combined, and then mix on high until the frosting is smooth and fluffy.

2 If your frosting is too goopy, add a little more powdered sugar. If it's too stiff, add some milk (just a teaspoon at a time).

Coconut Pecan

Ingredients

- 14-ounce can sweet-ened condensed milk (not evaporated milk)
- ½ cup water
- 3 egg yolks (See page 30.)
- 1 stick (½ cup) butter
- 1 teaspoon vanilla extract
- 1 cup pecans, chopped
- 2 cups sweetened coconut flakes
- pinch of salt

Equipment

- measuring cups and spoons
- can opener
- saucepot
- heat-proof rubber spatula

1 Stir the condensed milk, water, and egg yolks together in the saucepot. (Use the rubber spatula, not your finger, to get every last bit of condensed milk out of the can.) Add the butter and cook on medium heat, stirring occasionally, until the butter melts and the mixture bubbles.

2 Turn the stove down to low and cook another 5 minutes, stirring the whole time. Turn off the stove. Add the remaining ingredients and stir until everything is evenly combined.

3 Let the frosting cool a bit, but put it on the cake while it's still warm. Traditionally, this frosting doesn't go on the sides of the cake. If you want it to, double the recipe.

Lemon Glaze

Ingredients

- 1 cup powdered sugar
- juice of 1 lemon

Equipment

- measuring cup
- bowl
- fork

1 Stir the sugar and lemon juice together with the fork until the sugar dissolves.

2 Drizzle the glaze over warm cake.

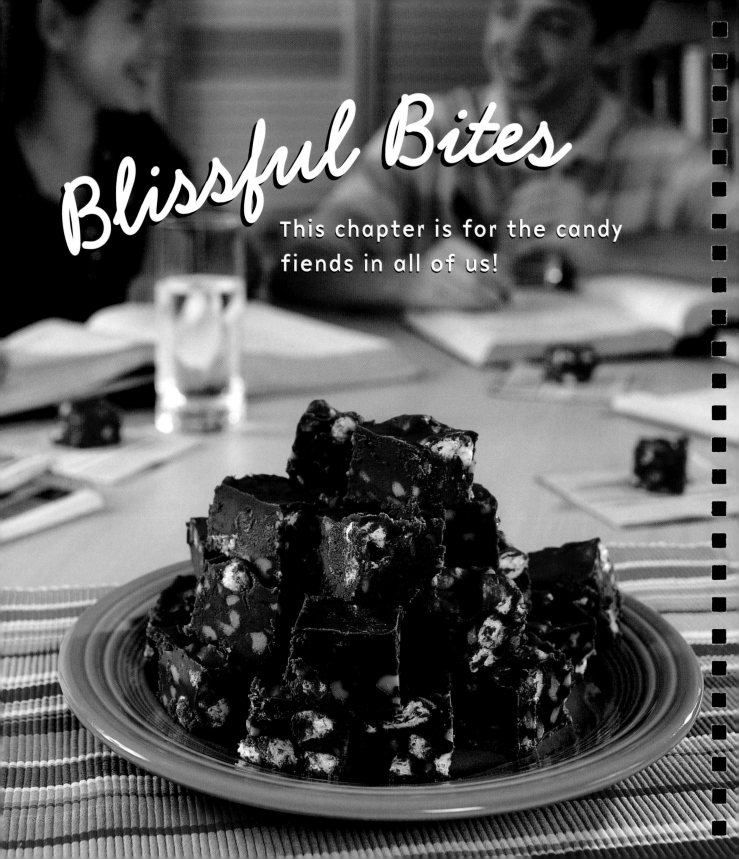

Blissful Bites

This chapter is for the candy fiends in all of us!

Rocky Road Fudge

This is some serious fudge! The recipe makes plenty to share, and it's a great holiday gift.

Equipment

• can opener • measuring cups and spoons • 2-quart saucepot (Don't use a smaller one or you'll have a boiling-over disaster.) • wooden spoon or heat-proof rubber spatula • helper (optional) • 9 x 13-inch baking dish, greased • plastic wrap • paring knife

Ingredients

- 7-ounce jar marshmallow fluff
- 5-ounce can evaporated milk (not condensed milk)
- 1½ cups sugar
- 1 stick (½ cup) butter
- ½ teaspoon salt
- 3 cups semisweet chocolate chips
- 1 teaspoon vanilla extract
- 1 cup chopped walnuts
- 2 cups mini marshmallows

Makes: 40 pieces of delectable fudge

You'll need about 20 minutes to make these treats and 2 hours for them to chill.

1 Melt the marshmallow fluff, evaporated milk, sugar, butter, and salt in the pot over medium heat. When the mixture boils, stir it until all the marshmallow fluff dissolves. (This will take 1 or 2 minutes.)

2 Turn off the stove and take the pot off the burner. Add the chocolate chips, and stir until they're melted. Stir in the vanilla extract. Fold the nuts and mini marshmallows into the chocolate goop.

3 Dump the mixture into the greased baking dish. (You might want to get a helper to hold the pot while you scrape every last bit into the dish.) Smooth the top with a rubber spatula or the back of a spoon. Let your helper lick the spoon. Cover the dish with plastic wrap.

4 Refrigerate the fudge for 2 hours, until firm. Cut the fudge into 1-inch squares. Enjoy!

Honey-Nut Baklava

Make this Mediterranean treat at home.

Ingredients

- ½ to 1 cup honey
- ½ cup water
- juice of half or a whole lemon
- 7 whole cloves
- 2 cups unsalted walnuts or pistachios
- 2 tablespoons sugar
- 1 stick (½ cup) butter, melted
- ½ pound phyllo dough, thawed according to the package directions

Makes: about 24 pieces

A.

B.

Equipment

- measuring cups and spoons • small saucepot • wooden spoon
- food processor or blender • pastry board • plastic wrap or waxed paper • greased baking dish the size of a sheet of phyllo
- pastry brush • paring knife • spoon

This dessert takes about 40 minutes to prepare and half an hour to bake.

1 Preheat the oven to 375°F. Put the nuts and sugar in the food processor. Pulse 20 to 30 times, until the nuts are coarsely ground.

2 Unroll the whole stack of thawed phyllo from its package. Lay it on your pastry board. Lay a piece of plastic wrap on top of the dough to keep it from drying out. Place the baking dish nearby.

3 Phyllo dough comes in sheets. Move the top sheet to the baking dish. Brush butter all over it. Put a second sheet on top. Brush butter on it. See photo A. Keep going for a total of 12 sheets. Don't worry about wrinkles or tears.

4 Spread the nut mixture over the phyllo. Layer the rest of the phyllo on top, buttering each sheet. Cut the baklava into diamond shapes. See photo B. Bake 25 to 30 minutes, until golden brown. Use oven mitts to remove it from the oven.

5 While the baklava bakes, combine the honey, water, lemon juice, and cloves in the saucepot. Bring to a boil. Reduce the heat to low. Simmer while you do everything else. Fish the cloves out of the honey syrup with a spoon. Slowly pour the syrup over the baked baklava. Let it cool before eating it!

Nutty Brittle

If you wear braces, just turn the page right now or be tortured with thoughts of this crispy, caramely, nutty candy. It'll get stuck in your teeth.

Equipment

- measuring cups and spoons • heavy-bottomed 4-quart saucepot (no smaller) • wooden spoon or heat-proof rubber spatula • cookie sheet, greased • oven mitts • helper • hot pads

Ingredients

- 1 cup sugar
- ½ cup corn syrup
- 1 cup nuts of your choice (If you choose almonds, go for slivered instead of sliced. The sliced ones tend to burn.)
- 1 tablespoon butter
- 1 teaspoon baking soda
- ¼ teaspoon salt (Leave it out if you're using salted nuts.)
- 1 teaspoon vanilla extract

Makes: about 1 pound of candy

You'll need about 20 minutes to make this candy, and 45 minutes for it to cool.

1 Stir the sugar and corn syrup together in the saucepot until the sugar is moistened. Add the nuts and butter. Bring to a boil over medium heat. This should take about 5 minutes. Be careful—don't get splattered with the boiling mixture.

2 Let the mixture boil for about 10 minutes as you stir it occasionally. When the color starts to change, turn off the stove and watch the mixture closely. It can quickly change from too light to perfect to burnt. Use oven mitts to take the saucepot off the burner as soon as the mixture is light amber. (See photo.) Err on the side of under-cooking the mixture.

3 Call your helper. Add the baking soda and salt. Carefully add the vanilla extract—it will sputter a bit when it hits the hot syrup. Stir the foaming mixture until everything is combined.

4 Wear oven mitts to pour the hot syrup onto the cookie sheet. Have your helper use a wooden spoon to scrape the last of it out of the saucepot. Use the back of the spoon to spread the molten mixture thinly over the sheet.

5 Let the candy cool for at least 45 minutes. (See page 31 for a trick to clean your pot.) Break the candy into pieces. Eat it, or store in a sealed container at room temperature.

Too-Cute Turtles

Are you too mature to pretend to be a lake monster emerging to crunch these defenseless, delicious turtles?

Equipment

- measuring cups • cookie sheet • oven mitts
- microwave-safe bowl • 2 small spoons

Ingredients

- 1½ cups pecan halves
- 14-ounce bag of old-fashioned cream caramels
- 1 cup chocolate chips

Makes: about 32 doomed turtles

You can be munching on these candies in half an hour.

1 Preheat the oven to 300°F. Arrange the pecan halves on the cookie sheet in Y-shaped clusters of three. (Look at the finished candies on the left to get the idea.)

2 Unwrap the caramels and place one on top of each group of nuts. Bake 10 to 12 minutes, until the caramels are slumped down over the nuts, but not oozing. Use oven mitts to remove the cookie sheet.

3 Put most of the chocolate chips in the bowl. (Save a little less than ¼ cup.) Microwave them on medium power for 1½ minutes. Take the bowl out and stir the melting chips. Microwave for another 30 seconds, and stir the chips again. Keep microwaving and stirring in 30 second increments until the chocolate is melted and shiny. Finally, add the chips that you saved, and stir until they melt.

4 Spoon melted chocolate over the caramel on each turtle. (I like to work with a spoon in each hand, so I can use one spoon to push the chocolate off the other.) Leave the tips of the nuts showing, like the turtle is sticking out its head and back legs.

5 Let the candy cool before you attack. I mean eat.

When Chocolate Misbehaves

Although following my steps for melting chocolate will help, chocolate chips are unpredictable when it comes to hardening. Goopy chocolate doesn't have to be a big deal. But if it is to you, you might have better luck using a 4-ounce semisweet chocolate bar, broken into chip-sized pieces.

Peanut Butter Balls

These delectable morsels are easy to make with kids you baby-sit. Try to decide which coating you like best.

Equipment

- measuring cups and spoons • mixing bowl • wooden spoon • shallow dish, such as a pie plate

Ingredients

- 1 cup peanut butter
- 1 cup powdered milk
- ½ cup honey
- ⅔ cup powdered sugar
- about 3 tablespoons chocolate sprinkles
- about ⅓ cup crispy rice cereal
- about ⅓ cup coconut flakes

Makes: about 30 balls

If you're fast, you can make these treats in 15 minutes. If you're babysitting, count on at least 30 minutes.

1 Combine the peanut butter, powdered milk, honey, and powdered sugar in the bowl. Stir until evenly blended. If your stirring arm gets tired, finish mixing with your hands. Roll the dough between your palms into balls about the size of a shooter marble.

2 Put the sprinkles in the shallow dish. Roll one third of the peanut butter balls, one at a time, in the sprinkles. You might need to press a little to make them stick. Roll another third of the balls in the cereal, and the rest in the coconut.

3 Refrigerate the candy for at least 20 minutes, until firm. Store leftover peanut butter balls in a sealed container in the fridge. Oh, who am I kidding? There won't be any leftovers.

Truffles

These bites of rich chocolate are named after a fungus. It's an extremely rare and delicious fungus. But still, a fungus. Go figure.

Equipment

- measuring cups and spoons • mixing bowl—microwave-safe, just in case • small saucepot
- whisk • plastic wrap • melon baller or small spoon • shallow dish, such as a pie plate

Ingredients

- two 4-ounce bars semisweet chocolate (The better quality the chocolate, the better the candy.)
- ½ cup heavy cream
- 1 teaspoon vanilla extract
- 1 teaspoon instant espresso or coffee (optional)
- about ¼ cup cocoa powder
- about ¼ cup powdered sugar

Makes: about 16 truffles

You'll work for less than half an hour to make these goodies, but they have to chill for an hour in the middle of it.

1. Break the chocolate into small pieces and put it in the bowl. Heat the cream and vanilla extract in the saucepot until it steams but doesn't bubble. Pour the hot cream over the chocolate. Let this mixture sit for a few minutes.

2. Whisk the mixture until the chocolate melts and mixes smoothly with the cream. (If the mixture doesn't get completely smooth, microwave it for 10 seconds and whisk some more.) This concoction is called ganache. Cover it with plastic wrap. Refrigerate for 1 hour.

3. Use a melon baller to scoop bite-sized chunks of ganache out of the bowl. Roll the chunks into spheres between your palms. If the ganache gets too goopy to roll into balls, put it back in the fridge for a while.

4. Put some cocoa powder in the shallow dish. Roll half of the truffles, one at a time, in the cocoa powder to coat. Roll the other half of the truffles in powdered sugar.

5. Truffles are best when you eat them at room temperature, but they should be stored in a sealed container in the refrigerator. Tell your little brother that those are just some weird fungi—who'd want to eat them?

Equipment Glossary

Serrated knife

Chef's knife

Paring knife

Wooden spoons

Spatula

Rubber spatulas

Whisk

Pastry blender

Sifter

Liquid measuring cup

Vegetable peeler

Corer

Measuring spoons

Scoop (dry) measuring cups

Grater

Skillet

Cutting/pastry boards

Electric mixer

Pots

Mixing bowls

Colander

Cooling rack

Food processor

Baking dish

Cookie/baking sheet

Glossary

Appliance: an electric tool such as a refrigerator, blender, or toaster.

Bake: cook in an oven. When the oven is set on "bake" the heat comes from the bottom of the oven and cooks food evenly from all sides.

Baking powder: a dry ingredient that makes baked foods rise. Read each recipe carefully—some use baking powder and some use baking soda. They are not the same thing!

Baking soda: a very strong dry ingredient that makes food puff up when it bakes. The scientific term for baking soda is sodium bicarbonate. It's a totally different ingredient than baking powder.

Beat: stir quickly with a fork, electric mixer, or whisk until well combined and a little bit fluffy.

Blender: an electric appliance for puréeing and other kinds of mixing.

Boil: what happens to a liquid when it gets hot enough to evaporate. It bubbles a lot.

Caramelize: heat sugar until it becomes an amber-colored syrup.

Colander: a piece of kitchen equipment that looks like a bowl with holes in it, used to rinse or drain foods.

Compote: fruit cooked in sugar syrup.

Cream: beat together softened butter and sugar. You could do this with a fork, but using an electric mixer is much easier and quicker.

Crumb layer: a thin layer of icing that traps cake crumbs.

Cutting board: a tool that protects your countertop from being cut by a knife.

Divide: to separate into more than one part.

Electric mixer: a great tool for mixing that keeps your arm from getting tired.

Equipment: another word for tools.

Flour: finely ground grain, usually wheat.

Fold: gently incorporate an ingredient into fluffy batter using a rubber spatula.

Fondant: a sugary mixture for coating cakes and decorating desserts.

Food processor: an appliance that helps you mix food, chop it, and more.

Ganache: an incredibly delicious mixture of chocolate and cream.

Grate: use a grater to cut food into small pieces.

Grater: a tool with small, sharp holes. You rub food such as a carrot against a grater to cut it into small pieces.

Grease: rub butter or oil on a baking pan so the food won't stick to it. I like to use the leftover butter wrapper for this.

Greased: what a pan is after you grease it.

Hot pad: a tool that you should use if you don't want to scorch your hands when you pick up hot pots and pans. Hot pads are usually padded squares of fabric.

Hull: remove the stem and leaves from fruit such as strawberries.

Ingredients: all the different foods that go into a recipe.

Liquid measuring cups: tools that are best at getting the perfect amount of a liquid ingredient such as milk.

Measuring spoons: tools for getting the right, small amount of an ingredient.

Mise en place: French for having your ingredients and equipment ready before you start cooking.

Offset spatula: a tool with a bent blade that's good for spreading.

Oven mitt: a tool that keeps you from burning your hands when you pick up hot pots and pans. Oven mitts are shaped so that you can slide your hand inside.

Pack: to squish an ingredient down into the measuring cup as you fill it. Brown sugar is typically packed when measuring it, but flour or other dry ingredients are not.

Paring knife: a small knife that's good for tiny, precise cuts. "Paring" means cutting the peel off of a fruit or vegetable, but I prefer a vegetable peeler for that job.

Pastry bag: a bag with a hole at one end used to make fancy icing decorations.

Peel: remove the skin of fruits and veggies.

Pick over: remove stems, bad pieces, or anything else you don't want to eat from berries.

Pinch: 1/16th of a teaspoon.

Preheat: letting the oven heat up to the right temperature before you bake in it. Some ovens have a preheat setting, but you just turn most to "bake."

Prep: getting ingredients ready before you start mixing up the recipe.

Produce: fresh fruits and vegetables.

Purée: blend into a smooth liquid or goo.

Recipe: a plan for making food.

Rind: the tough skin of fruit such as a honeydew.

Rubber spatula: a very useful mixing and spreading utensil.

Sift: push powdery ingredients through a sifter to remove lumps.

Sifter: a tool used to separate the fine particles of flour from the coarse particles.

Simmer: cook lightly in liquid that isn't quite boiling—there are a few small bubbles.

Slice: cut food into thin, flat pieces with a knife.

Soften: let an ingredient, such as butter, warm up to room temperature so it's squishy and easy to work with. Don't skip this important step.

Solid measuring cups: tools that are best at getting the perfect amount of a solid ingredient such as flour.

Spatula: a tool for turning and lifting food.

Sprinkles: tiny candy topping.

Stir: use a spoon to combine ingredients.

Substitute: an ingredient you can use instead of the one called for in the recipe.

Temper: add a little bit of a hot mixture to beaten eggs before adding the eggs to the whole mixture, so they don't curdle.

Trivet: sit a hot dish on one of these so that it doesn't burn the tabletop.

Utensil: a small tool with a handle.

Vegetable peeler: a tool that removes the peel of thin-skinned fruits and veggies.

Whip: mix food very fast to make a food such as icing super-fluffy.

Whipping cream: cream that gets big and fluffy when you whip it.

Whisk: the name of a tool, and the action of using it. Whisking uses a wrist motion to beat and/or smooth out lumps.

Yield: how many servings a recipe makes.

Zest: the colored part of the peel of citrus fruits such as oranges or lemons.

Metrics

Need to convert the measurements in this book to metrics? Here's how:

To convert degrees Fahrenheit to degrees Celsius, subtract 32 and then multiply by .56.

To convert inches to centimeters, multiply by 2.5.

To convert ounces to grams, multiply by 28.

To convert teaspoons to milliliters, multiply by 5.

To convert tablespoons to milliliters, multiply by 15.

To convert cups to liters, multiply by .24.

Acknowledgments

Big thanks to our models: Alex, Ben, Cecilia, Genevieve, Jen, Jules, Michaela, and Olivia. Thanks to Veronika, the wonder-editor. Thank you Robin, Skip, and John for making such a beautiful book. Thank you Marty, for introducing me to Strawberry Sticky; Liam, for manning the apple machine; and Steve, for your granita inspiration, taste-testing, and dishwashing. Also thanks to all the folks at Lark and Moog who made sure none of these sweet eats went to waste.

Index